IGNORE
AND
SCORE

HOW TO GET THE GIRL:
DATING MINDSETS EXPLAINED

Original design by ImageForce.ca

Edited by Jen Semchuk.

Version 1.7

Email me your dating questions at:
Questions@FullOfHateAndReadyToDate.com

Other work by Robert Belland:
GET THE GIRL - AN ONLINE VIDEO COURSE

Blog: *FullofHateAndReadyToDate.com*

TABLE OF CONTENTS

INTRODUCTION **1**
   YOU'RE ABOUT TO FEEL PAIN 1
   ABOUT IGNORE AND SCORE 2

MEET HER: ATTRACTION & LEADING **7**
   ABOUT THIS SECTION 7

CORE EMOTION: ATTRACTION **8**
   WHAT IS ATTRACTION? 8
   ATTRACTION IS APPLIED RESISTANCE. 9
   BUILDING TENSION 10
   SEDUCTION IS A GAME OF TUG-OF-WAR 12
   TENSION DO'S AND DON'TS 17

IGNORE **21**
   THE POWER OF YOUR ATTENTION. 21
   IGNORE YOUR GENETICS 22
   IGNORE REJECTION 23
   IGNORE HER BITCH SHIELD 25

SCORE. **29**
   SCORE CONFIDENCE. 29
   SCORE OPINIONS AND BOUNDARIES 31
   SCORE RESISTANCE 37
   RESIST JUMPING THROUGH HER HOOPS. 38

CORE BEHAVIOR: LEADING **43**
   WHAT IS LEADING? 43

IGNORE **48**
   IGNORE YOUR INSECURITIES 48
   IGNORE YOUR FRIENDS AND FAMILY 51
   IGNORE YOUR PAST DATING MISTAKES 53
   IGNORE YOUR FEARS 54

SCORE. **57**
   SCORE YOUR OWN APPROVAL 57
   STOP JUDGING YOURSELF AND OTHERS 58

KEEP HER: RAPPORT & ESCALATION **61**
   ABOUT THIS SECTION 61

CORE EMOTION: RAPPORT **62**
   WHAT IS RAPPORT? 62
   WHEN IS THE RIGHT TIME TO BUILD RAPPORT? 64
   HOW DO WE BUILD RAPPORT? 66
   CONNECT THROUGH STORYTELLING 68

IGNORE **71**
   UNDERSTAND AND ALLAY HER RESISTANCE 71
   REMOVING HER RESISTANCE 73
   PUSH/PULL DYNAMIC 76
   IGNORE YOUR JEALOUSY AND LEARN FROM IT 78
   IGNORE HER TESTS 81

SCORE. **84**
   SCORE INDICATORS OF INTEREST 84
   SCORE BANTER 89
   SCORE FUN: BANTER AND ROLE-PLAYING 93
   SCORE CONGRUENCE 95
   SCORE BOUNDARIES 96
   SCORE YOUR OWN PURPOSE 101

CORE BEHAVIOUR: ESCALATION. **104**
   WHAT IS ESCALATION? 104

IGNORE **108**
   IGNORE YOUR URGE TO GO FAST. 108
   IGNORE YOUR DESIRE TO BE DIRECT 109
   IGNORE YOUR INSECURE REACTIONS 111

SCORE. **115**
   SCORE INTIMACY. 115
   SCORE VULNERABILITY. 116
   SCORE SEXUAL INTIMACY 121
   SCORE TRUST THROUGH ESCALATION 123
   LET DOWN YOUR GUARD IN THE BEDROOM. 125

CONCLUSION **127**
   FINAL THOUGHTS 127

MAILBAG QUESTIONS & ANSWERS **131**
   ABOUT THIS SECTION. 131

GYM FLIRTING AND PICKUP? **132**

FIRST DATE ADVICE? **136**

IS BEING DESPERATE THE SAME AS WANTING A RELATIONSHIP? **144**

NUMBER FIRST OR DATE FIRST? **148**

HOW SIMPLE IS IT TO GET A GIRLFRIEND? **150**

WAS I BEING WUSSY? **153**

I MISS HER, WHAT CAN I DO? **157**

FIRST DATE LOCATION? **161**

GET A SECOND CHANCE? **163**

DOES IGNORING GIRLS REALLY WORK? **165**

BEST WAY TO APPROACH A GIRL? **168**

FINAL THOUGHTS READ THIS FIRST 173
A Letter To Myself 173

RESOURCES & LINKS. 192
LINKS 192

INTRODUCTION

YOU'RE ABOUT TO FEEL PAIN

Getting the girl isn't just a Hollywood fantasy; attracting beautiful women isn't the sole domain of the super rich, the super hunk, or the outrageously gifted. I know this now, but for most of my life, I believed the opposite, as well as other crippling assumptions about women, dating, and sex.

I'm writing this book for my fellow man because I was once where you are: confused, frustrated, and lonely.

Here's a painful truth: The average guy will never choose the woman he wants.

Why? you may ask. It's simple: Most men will never act outside the box—the "box" being the habitual beliefs and attitudes we take for granted about ourselves and the world.

It's true: Pain may be ahead for you if you choose to rethink your attitudes and beliefs about women, dating, attraction, and relationships. Changing your attitudes and behaviours is hard to do because we normally don't like to step beyond what is comfortable and we think what we know is beyond question.

This is not a journey for the weak. Questioning what we take for granted and trying new things outside of our comfort zones just might be the hardest things we can do, but I believe this capacity to change is what truly makes us human.

And if you're brave enough to buy a book like this, then you're already on a journey that most men will never take.
On this journey, you will no doubt encounter some surprises, such as:

- Nice guys without personal boundaries do finish last.
- Putting her on a pedestal will not get you the girl.
- Tension is necessary for attraction.
- Dating is not all about her expectations; your expectations should count more to you.
- Seduction is a tug-of-war.
- Body language and tone of voice constitute 93% of communication; what you actually say accounts for the other 7%.
- Your self-esteem and life passions are tantamount to getting the girl.
- A woman may reject or resist you and still want you—you just have to know when to keep pursuing and when to quit.

If you want a new life with new women, you must think about and try new things. This eBook is all about you rewriting your beliefs and attitudes and adopting new behaviours. If you want to succeed with women and learn some new life lessons along the way, read on!

ABOUT IGNORE AND SCORE

The title of this book came to me when I was paying attention to a table of beautiful young women sitting across from me in a restaurant. I was surprised by the body language of the men the young women were sitting with. The guys looked indifferent and bored. While the women were leaning into the men and vying for their attention, the guys were actively chatting with each other and ignoring them.

I just didn't get it! If I was in the position of one of these men, I would give my date all the attention she would ever want.

After that, I started paying more attention to the way couples behaved in public. I soon noticed this behaviour everywhere. Guys with hot girlfriends seemed almost bored with them. In fact, it appeared as if the more the guy ignored his girlfriend, the more interested the girlfriend seemed.

My friend Mike and I nicknamed this phenomenon *Ignore and Score*. It was our way of mocking what we didn't understand at the time.

About a year later, I came across the following quote rather serendipitously while doing some research on dating dynamics:

> *"Show me a beautiful woman and I'll show you a man who's tired of fucking her."*

Then I got it: The reason why some guys ignore and score is actually anti-intuitive and surprising.

First, I want you to understand that my original definition of Ignore and Score was misguided. You can't simply ignore a woman and expect to score her attention, attraction, or affection.

Rather, the term Ignore and Score represents behaviours and attitudes that naturally trigger a woman's attention and ultimately her attraction.

You'll discover that when you ignore specific beliefs, attitudes, and behaviours, your dating life will improve. In other words, by learning to ignore certain things, you'll score what you want.

So, ignore has two meanings here—what you must overcome and what you must avoid in order to be more attractive to women. Score also has two meanings—what you personally gain from changing attitudes, beliefs, or behaviours and what you need to develop and focus on in order to succeed with women.

Ignore and Score is broken into two sections: **Meet Her** and **Keep Her.**

Meet Her is about first contact and how your leading behaviours can encourage a woman's to find you attractive.

Keep Her is about connection and how your escalating behaviours move a relationship from simple attraction to the deeper intimacy of rapport.

Here's your first lesson: What drives every decision a woman makes in her life time?

The answer is **<u>emotional expectation.</u>**

This is the same for us guys—every decision we make is intended to have some type of impact on how we feel.

A woman chooses a certain guy because she expects that being with him will make her feel a certain way. We'll learn what these expectations are and how you can be attractive in this regard, but don't be mistaken—this is not about changing yourself to suit the whims and wants of any given woman. In fact, as we will see, being attractive and building rapport with a woman means **being your own man.** We'll look at what this means as you read along.

✍ **Go Online For Resources & Links For This Section:**
www.IgnoreAndScore.com/intro

Questions about This Section? Email Me Here:
questions@IgnoreAndScore.com

MEET HER: ATTRACTION & LEADING

ABOUT THIS SECTION

This section discusses the two essential factors in meeting women: attraction and leading. Attraction is the core emotion you want to arouse in a woman; to be attractive, you need to behave like a leader—behaving like a leader is all about a change of mindset. You're not merely the pursuer, you are also the prize. This is the game of seduction that will have women pursuing you.

CORE EMOTION: ATTRACTION

WHAT IS ATTRACTION?

Attraction is the first of two core emotions required for successful dating; the second is **rapport** and will be discussed later in the context of building a more lasting connection with a woman.

Attraction is all about **tension**.

Understanding this will forever change how you interact with women.

Without tension, there can be *no* attraction.

What is this tension we feel when we're attracted to a woman?

Tension is defined by the space between where you are (e.g., meeting a woman for the first time) and where you want to be (e.g., in bed with her).

This electrified space between reality and fantasy is tension. Tension is the necessary corollary of attraction.

This is why you don't want what you already have. The space

between wanting it and having it is gone, and tension is lost. On the other hand, wanting what you have no hope of getting also makes for negligible tension. If a woman is super hot but unattainable, there can be very little tension created between you.

Most men are attracted to a woman based entirely on how she looks. Be careful here. If you're driven to date women simply because they're beautiful, you'll discover that attraction based simply on looks doesn't last because the tension between you cannot be maintained.

You might be saying, *"But Robby, I've always hated tension because it feels awful, so won't it make her feel awful too?"*

The reality is that tension isn't necessarily good or bad; tension is just a feeling. It's how we *interpret* our tension that makes it good or bad. If you anticipate something good happening, your brain will label your tension as 'good.' If you anticipate something terrible, your brain will label your tension 'bad' and seek to diminish it.

Creating tension in a relationship with a woman is a fine balance of keeping up a sense of mystery and unpredictability about yourself as well as maintaining your personal boundaries, while ensuring your date doesn't interpret the tension she feels as a warning sign of possible danger.

ATTRACTION IS APPLIED RESISTANCE

Tension is created when a force is applied; that force is **resistance.** If you give your date *exactly* what she wants, *all* of the time, you're effectively killing her attraction for you.

Women are not attracted to "nice guys" because nice guys actively try to rid themselves of tension by endlessly agreeing and apologizing. What nice guys don't realize is that attraction is tension.

The attraction a woman feels for you is her emotional anticipation of who you are and how she expects you'll make her feel.

Attraction is an emotion and is, therefore, generally speaking, out of our conscious control. As dating guru David DeAngelo says, *"Attraction isn't a choice."* Just as we have instincts to Fight or Flight, we have instincts to Fuck or Chuck. If you understand that a woman's attraction to you is based on a kind of instinctual feeling, you'll be 99% further ahead than most other men.

Your job is to build a woman's interest and anticipation by letting her know how fun, honest, sincere, intelligent, and caring you are while also giving her some resistance to gaining full access to you. This resistance is the tension she'll enjoy, and it's the basis of her growing attraction to you.

If there's no resistance, either because you're unavailable (married, gay, uninterested) or because you're *overly* available, (nice, transparent guy with no boundaries), any attraction she may have felt for you simply dies off.

BUILDING TENSION

We don't want what we have; we want what's just out of reach.

Give a girl what she wants, without resistance, and you'll extinguish her attraction. If you tease a woman by interchangeably giving and withholding, you build tension and attraction.

Relationships often fail when those involved get exactly what they want when they want it. Give a woman perfect certainty and her desire will fade; give a woman hope *and* uncertainty, and she'll want you forever.

Let's look at a pick-up line that doesn't work because it doesn't create tension:

> *"Wow, you have the most amazing eyes I've ever seen...*
> *wow, you're so beautiful. Can I buy you a drink!?"*

Why don't beautiful women respond to compliments? Because you're not the first guy to notice she has beautiful eyes or amazing hair or great legs. The fact that you think you're the first guy to compliment her will communicate to her that you're just like every other arrogant, hotheaded guy.

When you drown a woman in compliments and put her on a pedestal, you're displaying **low personal value.**

Beautiful women *desire* resistance from men but rarely get it.

How about using the following twist on an otherwise unsurprising compliment:

> *"Wow, you have beautiful eyes...except for the left one."*
> *(*wink*)*

If you can make a woman laugh, she'll link her pleasure with your company. Pull her in with humour but push her away a little, too:

> *"Wow, you are so beautiful! You'll make all the other*
> *women jealous."*

Teasing like this communicates to a woman that she's desired but can't use your vulnerability to walk all over you.

It's this combination of pushing her away and pulling her in that creates tension, and tension is the core of what builds and maintains attraction. Creating tension in the context of dating is the game of seduction.

SEDUCTION IS A GAME OF TUG-OF-WAR

Seduction is like a game of tug-of-war between you and a woman.

What outcome do you think the woman wants?

Imagine that you simply pull as hard as you can on the rope and the woman falls right into your arms:

> **YOU:** *"Wow, you're so beautiful! Can I buy you a drink? Will you give me your number? Are you single? Please be single! My roommate's gone; wanna come back to my place?"*

This is frustrating for the woman because she has no chance to pull you back, and the game is over in seconds. When you show her all of your cards, or when you barrage her with your compliments and desires, she'll be overwhelmed and won't feel like she has any room to play. That's boring and predictable.

Furthermore, if you're fast and impatient when playing the game of attraction, she'll assume you're just as impatient in the bedroom.

Letting her win easily presents similar problems:

> **HER:** *"Hey, my name's Brenda. Umm... so what brings you out tonight?"*

> **YOU:** *"Hey, Brenda! Can I buy you a drink! Oh, I love your purse! Hey, Steve, beat it so Brenda can sit there! So Brenda, I'm single, and I think you're sooo hot. Wanna go back to my*

place?"

When you become instantly available to her flirting, she'll suspect you have low personal value, and she'll feel her victory is empty. If you let her easily win, she'll have no investment in further play.

When you play the dating game, like when you play tug-of-war, you must be resistant enough to make the game enjoyable and to facilitate her investment in the process.

If it's all pull, it's boring; if there's no pull, it's not worth it. But if there's **pull and push**, it's GOLD!

YOU: *"Hey, I'm Steve."*

HER: *"Hey, Steve, I'm Brenda."*

YOU: *"Hey, Brenda, I just came over here because I thought you had such a cute smile! But I have the impression you're kinda bratty, so I figured I'd come over here and see for myself. Hey, actually, those are decent shoes! I love flats."*

HER: *"Hahaha, bratty, eh? What? My shoes? Oh ya, pretty sweet, eh? It's one of those casual days for me. Usually I'm in heels actually, so you've caught me on a good day, I suppose."*

YOU: *"Oh no! Are you one of those girls who wears those high heels with the really weird pointy toes? Those things totally creep me out! Ha ha."*

HER: *"Ha ha ha! Ya, I love those shoes! What's wrong with those shoes?"*

YOU: *"Well... you know what they say about girls who wear those shoes right? (*wink*) Wait a minute, you have the cutest accent. Let me guess... you grew up around here?"*

HER: *"What do they say about girls who wear those shoes? Don't skip right over that!" (*pushes you*)*

YOU: *"Yup. You were born here, I can tell. You actually make it sound good. Let me guess, you're either an accountant or a dentist's assistant."*

The mistake most guys make when they meet a girl is that they think they need to overdo it with the pull, but the reality is that this just pushes women away.

Attraction isn't all about pulling her in with your wit, your looks, your money, or your charm; it's also about the emotional energy of anticipation and mystery.

I'll give you three scenarios in which a man approaches a woman and uses 1) only pull, 2) only resistance, and 3) both pull and resistance:

Scenario 1 – PULL:

DICK: *"Hi. My name's Dick."*

JANE: *"Hi, Dick. I'm Jane."*

DICK: *"Wow, I think you're beautiful, Jane."*

JANE: *"Oh, wow, thanks!"*

DICK: *"Seriously. You have the most beautiful eyes! Are you a model?"*

JANE: *"Um, thanks. No, I'm a dentist actually."*

DICK: *"That's great. That explains why you have the most perfect teeth I've ever seen. Can I buy you a drink?"*

JANE: *"Um, no thanks. I'm just waiting for my friend actually."*

DICK: *"Oh, okay."*

Notice how Dick showed how interested he was by showering her with compliments. This doesn't work because it was all pull. A man of greater value would want to get to know her a little more before deciding how he feels about her.

You can almost imagine Dick invisibly trying to pull Jane into his game of tug-of-war; this behaviour makes Dick seem shallow and insecure and makes Jane disinterested in even taking up her end of the rope.

Sometimes when you're trying to pull a girl in, you find you'll start to physically lean into her; her automatic response to having a man lean into her would be to lean away.

Pay attention to your physical posturing when chatting with women: be sure to never lean into them for more than a few moments. Try to always be leaning away; you'll notice that if she's interested, she'll start leaning into you instead.

Scenario 2 – RESISTANCE:

DICK: *"Hi. My name's Dick."*

JANE: *"Hi, Dick. I'm Jane."*

DICK: *"Wow, that's a lame name."*

JANE: *"Ha ha, what? Ya, Dick's pretty original, too, eh?"*

DICK: *"Hey, what's with the blouse?"*

JANE: *"What? What do you mean?"*

DICK: *"Well, look at it. Seriously? Whatever. So, you're here trying to pick up men? Looks like you need some help. I'd suggest trying a little makeup and maybe hit the gym once in a while."*

JANE: *"Ya, um, how about you get lost, loser. Hey, Todd, can you get this guy out of here?"*

This time, all Dick was doing was pushing her away. Pure resistance without any pull communicates to a woman that you are disinterested or you're just a jackass.

Be careful when you're trying to be cocky; sometimes cocky can come across harshly and be interpreted as pure resistance on your part. If you can't be funny when you're acting cocky, drop the act!

Scenario 3 – PULL AND RESISTANCE:

DICK: *"Hi. My name's Dick."*

JANE: *"Hi, Dick. I'm Jane."*

DICK: *"You have the most beautiful eyes!"*

JANE: *"Oh, well, thanks."*

DICK: *"Especially the left one."*

JANE: *"Haha, shut up!"*

DICK: *"I'm actually just waiting for my buddy, so I'll likely have to run away from you in a moment, I just wanted to come over and say hi. He hates it when I flirt with anyone;*

he gets so jealous." (*wink*)

JANE: *"Ha, well, thanks, I guess. Run away from me, eh?"*

DICK: *"You seem pretty harmless – so far. If you're not dangerous, you're welcome to come sit with us."*

JANE: *"Ha, well, I am very dangerous actually."*

DICK: *"Haha, ya, I got that feeling when I saw you eyeballing me when I came in here."*

JANE: *"Ha ha, WHAT?! I did not!"*

DICK: *"Jane. Please. We both know how this works. I've seen Dateline. I know a stalker when I see one. But don't sweat it – I think you're a pretty cute stalker."*

JANE: *"Ha ha. You saw right through me. I'm impressed, Dick."*

This time Dick added humour (pull) to his teasing (resistance). Jane knows Dick's being playful, and this communicates to her that he is fun, smart, and confident. This kind of teasing and role-playing is called **banter**, and we'll discuss it more in a later chapter on developing rapport.

TENSION DO'S AND DON'TS

Here is a list of things to remember when building good tension with a woman:

   👎 **DON'T LAUGH TOO MUCH.** Uncomfortable laughter is our body's way of releasing tension. This might be a good thing if you're trying to avoid getting punched in the face right before a bar fight, but it won't go far when you're trying to seduce a woman. Don't be that guy who laughs at his own jokes or who laughs more than everyone else. Learn to accept and appreciate the added tension that not laughing wildly or inappropriately brings.

👍 **TALK SLOWER.** When we're nervous, we unconsciously start to talk too quickly. Some people even stutter. Take a deep breath and simply allow the tension to exist without you needing to reduce it. If you talk nice and slow, women will perceive you as a calm, cool guy rather than a nervous wreck whom she can write off.

👎 **DON'T FIDGET, ROCK, OR BITE YOUR NAILS.** We all have nervous habits that help us control the tension in our bodies. If you want to lessen the tension of a situation, learn to breathe deeply and control your own behaviours. Meditation is a great tool for calming your own nerves. Calm your body using meditative techniques not by relying on off-putting nervous ticks.

👎 **DON'T APOLOGIZE FOR EVERYTHING.** Apologizing too much communicates to a woman that you're insecure and require her constant approval and/or forgiveness. Women don't want emotionally needy men. Learn to control and deal with your own insecurities.

👎 **DON'T LIE.** Sometimes we feel the truth will create too much tension, but the reality is that unexpected honesty creates the best kind of tension.

👎 **DON'T HIDE YOURSELF.** Sometimes we become intimidated by those around us, and in an unconscious effort to avoid conflict and tension, we shrink ourselves. Instead of hiding yourself, build your courage and express yourself. Take up space. When sitting with friends, let your arms and legs fill your personal space. Take up room. Make your person matter.

🖘 **DON'T FROWN OR SNEER.** If you like what you see, then smile—it's friendly and nice. The guy who doesn't smile is creepy and unfriendly.

👍 **SPEAK CLEARLY AND WITH AUTHORITY.** If she has to say "What?" because she didn't hear what you said, you're letting tension slip away. Speak clearly. For full effect, shift from loud to soft depending on the story but always make sure you're heard. This behaviour will force her to listen more carefully. Changing between louder and softer tones helps build a woman's interest and attraction by requiring her to interchangeably focus when you speak more softly and relax when you speak more loudly.

👍 **HOLD STRONG EYE CONTACT, AT FIRST.** When we're nervous, we unintentionally break eye contact. Don't do this when you first interact with her. It's okay to look around casually, but be sure to keep strong eye contact whenever suitable. It communicates that you're confident.

Focusing our attention on a woman without breaking eye contact has the potential of making her feel uncomfortable. It's more useful to give her your total attention in short spurts, so that she can experience the pleasure of your undivided attention but also the pleasure of its release. This is another instance of keeping it fun by creating a rhythm of push and pull.

👍 **BE CALM AND COMPOSED.** Don't react emotionally to any nervousness she may be displaying. By remaining calm and smiling comfortably, you'll inspire her to relax and to feel calm as well. It's an unconscious way of leading her: if you smile, she'll smile; if you're calm, she'll feel calm. She might be high strung, and the more into you she becomes, the more she'll become bouncy, high energy, and nervous.

When you're composed, you're communicating that she doesn't make you nervous. This composure helps lead her to believe you're confident and that you feel you are of value.

 KEEPS STRONG, POSITIVE, AND CONFIDENT BODY LANGUAGE. Moving slowly indicates that you're composed and confident, which helps her relax and shows her you're confident despite the tension of the situation. Pay attention to how you stand, sit, and generally move. Your nervousness will show, and you'll transfer it onto her.

If you want to learn about powerful, confident male body language, rent the Ocean's Eleven movies and watch how Brad Pitt and George Clooney carry themselves. The goal is to always be comfortable and relaxed in all of your body movements. Move slowly and deliberately, even if it feels forced and overly-dramatic; the more you do it, the more natural it will feel.

IGNORE

THE POWER OF YOUR ATTENTION

What is attention?

It's the focus of your thinking and awareness. We pay attention to the road when we want to avoid dangers on the road; we pay attention in class when we want to learn what's being taught.

At a young age, we're taught to pay attention, generally through a reward and punishment system. In the past, when you paid attention, you were rewarded; for example, a girlfriend appreciated when you listened to her and she said: *"You really hear me."* When you didn't pay attention, you were punished or ridiculed; for example, you were judged to be a loser if you didn't pay attention to certain social conventions or fashions.

The ultimate punishment is social rejection: **being ignored or ridiculed by others**. This applies to both children and adults.

As an adult, certain givens, negative self-assessments, and fears don't serve you and, in fact, may keep you from accomplishing important goals in your life. What you pay attention to (e.g., fears and insecurities) may be disempowering you. Certain fears and insecurities need to be expunged so you can turn your attention to what can empower you in the realm of dating. We'll turn to what you should "ignore" and "score" next.

IGNORE YOUR GENETICS

You can't do anything about your genes. Some of us are going to be naturally taller, shorter, fatter, or thinner; you may be born with great hair and wonderful skin or stringy hair and acne.

But you're lucky because any man can look good, even if he's not good-looking. Women don't choose whom they're attracted to based on a man's God-given attributes. Attraction is a completely emotional response which she'll rationalize later.

For these reasons, you need to focus only on the parts of yourself that will score the greatest impact on her emotionally.

A woman will likely assess the following about you when she first sees you:

- Recognition (Do I know him?)

- Safety (Is he creepy or does he seem trustworthy? Will he hurt me?)

- Social impact (Will he embarrass me? Will he make me look good? Will he lower or add to my status?)

- Emotional impact (Will he make me feel good? Is he fun?)

- Sexual parity (Does he have "good genes," provider traits, social influence, sexual confidence, and competence?)

In other words, a woman is attracted to you for other, more important reasons than simple physicality; she is attracted to your personality, intelligence, character, sense of humour, daddy-potential—everything she finds attractive about you makes her feel good when she's with you.

Your appearance comes down to the following: 1) **hygiene**

(it trumps everything); 2) **safety** (do you look dangerous or creepy?); and 3) **confidence** (body language, how you define your own boundaries, and how others are responding to you).

When it comes to hygiene:

- 👍 If your teeth are yellow, whiten them. Whitening costs about $40 but has an amazing impact on your smile.

- 👍 If your breath is bad, brush your teeth and use breath mints.

- 👍 If you grow body hair like an ape, keep it trimmed, shaved, or waxed.

Your appearance is something you can manage and refine.

Later, we'll talk about how you can project safety and confidence.

Remember: You don't have to be good-looking to look good; you don't have to be handsome to be *sexy*.

IGNORE REJECTION

Why does rejection scare us so much? Because our ancestors were taught that rejection by females and/or social groups affected the gene pool and ultimately meant death. Those ancestors who feared rejection avoided it, thereby making you possible.

We also learned fear of rejection from peers and television— both being powerful vehicles of conformity. But we won't play a blaming game here; instead, let's take this opportunity to re-educate ourselves about what rejection by a woman actually means.

Have you ever really thought about all of the reasons a woman might not be interested in a relationship with you?

At first, you're likely to put all of the blame onto yourself. You may think, for instance, "I'm just not [insert: "attractive," "rich," or "funny" here] enough."

All of this blame comes from your ego in a kind of survival mode where you avoid risks to protect yourself from ridicule and failure. If you allow risk-aversion, rather than growth, to define the way you relate to the world, you'll end up stuck in a cycle of approval-seeking and avoidance.

Once you've spent some time away from your risk-averse ego, you'll realize that women have endless reasons for not being available to your dating advances, such as:

- She's got a boyfriend.

- She's lesbian.

- Her Dad just died and she's very sad.

- Her new red shoes don't fit so she's really pissed off about it.

- She had so much sex this weekend that she's just not in the mood for more.

- She smelled her own fart before you approached her, and it ruined her mood.

- She's too nervous about making a mistake in front of you and decided not to risk her own rejection by rejecting you first.

- She doesn't like men who wear jackets.

- She's actually interested but far too shy to show it.

- She's testing you by being a bitch (more on this later).

- She's hoping you'll go away so the hot guy behind you comes over.

- She's worried her friends will think she's a slut if she talks to you.

- Her best friend wants you so she's stepping aside so her friend can have a chance.

- Et cetera...

With a million possible reasons why any given woman at any given time under any given circumstance might not want to engage in a conversation with you, automatically assuming the worst is not fair to yourself, plus a self-defeating attitude will ensure you don't have a chance with any woman.

Women have their own reasons for not engaging us in conversation and, ultimately, it's none of our business why. So relax! Her reasons for rejecting you almost always have nothing to do with you or what you can reasonably control. What really matters is how you choose to feel about it.

IGNORE HER BITCH SHIELD

Women are just as nervous about being rejected as you are.

But a woman's got far more to worry about when you approach her than a bruised ego.

Women need to keep themselves safe, in a way that most men

will never appreciate, so most beautiful women have a defense mechanism that's sometimes called a "bitch shield." This defense helps a woman keep potential weirdo's at bay and may sometimes be applied indiscriminately to the average, well-meaning guy who's gotten up the nerve to try and talk to her.

The bitch shield may be expressed as a look of disgust or annoyance, but most women will simply act unresponsive to your initial attempt at engaging them. Most women don't have it in them to be completely rude; instead, they simply won't give you any attention. Their hope is that you'll just go away.

While most guys feel angry or rejected when a woman ignores them or gives them a bad look, you now recognize another possibility for her behaviour: It's her natural defense mechanism at work.

If you continue to lead the interaction despite her initial lack of interest, you may just succeed in piquing her interest. Of course, it's also important to know when to quit, keeping in mind the many reasons why she may be disinterested in you (see under "Ignore Rejection" above).

Here's a great example from the movie Vicky Cristina Barcelona; in this scene, Juan Antonio demonstrates the kind of confidence you need when confronted by a woman's (here, Cristina's) suspicion or indifference:

JUAN ANTONIO: *"American?"*

CRISTINA: *"I'm Cristina, and this is my friend Vicky."*

JUAN ANTONIO: *"What color are your eyes?"*

CRISTINA: *"Uh, they're blue."*

JUAN ANTONIO: *"Well, I'd like to invite you both to come with me to Oviedo."*

VICKY: *"To come where?"*

JUAN ANTONIO: *"To Oviedo. For the weekend. We leave in one hour."*

CRISTINA: *"What ... Where is Oviedo?"*

JUAN ANTONIO: *"A very short flight."*

VICKY: *"By plane?"*

JUAN ANTONIO: *"Mm-hm."*

CRISTINA: *"What's in Oviedo?"*

JUAN ANTONIO: *"I go to see a sculpture that is very inspiring to me. A very beautiful sculpture. You will love it."*

VICKY: *"Oh, right. You're asking us to fly to Oviedo and back."*

JUAN ANTONIO: *"Mm. No, we'll spend the weekend. I mean, I'll show you around the city, and we'll eat well. We'll drink good wine. We'll make love."*

VICKY: *"Yeah, who exactly is going to make love?"*

JUAN ANTONIO: *"Hopefully, the three of us."*

Juan Antonio (played by Javier Bardem) is a man so deeply in touch with a woman's needs that he's effortlessly able to seduce any woman he desires. Watch the movie and pay close attention to how Juan *ignores* the pessimistic behaviours of the women he

seduces, only to eventually *score* each of their interests.
Women generally don't make decisions based on deep intellec-
tual debate because women are just like you and me: they make
decisions based upon how they *feel*.

How she feels is *everything*. Feelings are persuasive and
contagious. If you saunter over to a woman you're interested
in, whether at the bar, the corner store, or the laundry mat,
don't instantly crumble when she responds to your initial
contact with disinterest or distrust.

SCORE

SCORE CONFIDENCE

Did you know that darkness isn't real?

Wait, I can already hear you arguing with me. But think about this: If I asked you to bring me some darkness what would you do?

You see, darkness is really the absence of light; it has no reality in and of itself. This is an important idea.

Let's say you're in a room with absolutely no light; how much light would it take to destroy the perfect dark?

Any amount of light would, even one single match.

What does this have to do with confidence?

What if we can think of our **insecurities** as having no intrinsic reality, just as darkness has no inherent reality except as an absence of light. Shine a light of confidence into the stultifying darkness and your insecurities lose their power over you. The more light you shine, the more your insecurities are diminished.

Buddhists describe the mind as a mirror. A mirror, like the mind, reflects everything around it, but over time, dust accumulates on the mirror which distorts what is reflected. This is why Buddhists think it's important to always be "polishing the mirror" so as to maintain **clarity of mind**, free of distortions.

I'm going to go one step further: I've come to believe that we're born innately confident. Not some level of confident, just simply confident, completely free of shame and fear.

When you think about it, the idea that we develop confidence is ridiculous. That's like saying we learn to be alive or learn to grow hair. I believe we're all intrinsically confident, and we learn to feel insecure. We all have dust on our mirrors and a few footprints too.

Insecurities are like thousands of distracting little voices that destroy our natural state of confidence and peace. It is a mistake to conclude "I just need to develop my confidence," because you are basically saying your insecurities have an antecedent reality to your innate confidence.

Confidence isn't a muscle you can build; it's not something you're missing, and it's not something someone else can give to you or take from you. You always have it; it's always there, and it's never going away. The real problem is that insecurities distract us from appreciating the power of our intrinsic state of confidence.

Our job as men is to learn how to get rid of disempowering voices inhibiting our intrinsic calm and initiative. Our goal isn't to build confidence because we already have it. Our goal is to remove the negative, disempowering voices that distract and hinder us in order to regain control of ourselves and our destinies.

Remember the old saying, "You get more of what you focus on?" What we think about gets our attention; what gets our attention gains influence over us. It's time to be aware of how we're allowing ourselves to be influenced.

Remember when you bought your first car? For argument's sake, it was a Honda Accord. Then for the next month, all you noticed on the streets were other Honda Accords. This isn't because everyone in your town suddenly ran out and bought Honda Accords; it's because your mind was on your new car, and your attention was suddenly focused on Honda Accords.

If our focus is on having more confidence, we're wasting time and energy on a misguided goal.

Instead, I propose the following:

1. Stop resisting your insecurities as if they have more power and reality than your confidence; if you fight them, you only empower them.

2. Insecurities are like dirt on your mirror. If you're filtering your reality through dirt, all you're going see in life is dirt. Acknowledge the insecurity and separate it from yourself. Doing so polishes your mirror.

3. Identify with your intrinsic confidence and show it.

SCORE OPINIONS AND BOUNDARIES

Have you ever been this guy?

SALLY: *"Oh, man, I hate this song! The Barenaked Ladies are so terrible!"*

BRAD: *"Oh, ya, I hate them too; they're so bad, right?"*

SALLY: *"I didn't know you hated them, too. Who do you listen to, then?"*

BRAD: *"Oh, I don't know. I like all music, I guess."*
SALLY: *"Oh. Well, where should we go eat? What do you like to eat?"*

BRAD: *"Oh, I don't know. I guess I like everything."*

SALLY: *"I love Chinese, how about that?"*

BRAD: *"Oh, ya, I love Chinese; that sounds great!"*

This is the kind of guy that women hate.

He's too agreeable. He latches onto her likes and dislikes so as to not cause any friction, not understanding that it takes friction (resistance) to create attraction.

Being generic is boring and undermines your chance of developing something new and fun because women tend to ignore men who are predictable and overly-agreeable.

You must define yourself for yourself.

Have you ever been that guy who really likes a girl and out of fear of rejection becomes Mr. Generic? This is the guy who'll morph his preferences to match hers with the expectation she'll respond more positively to him if they share a bunch of opinions or tastes.

Women can tell you're either being a phony kiss ass (because you're trying to get something from her: approval or sex) or you're too insecure to express your own point of view.

Women are attracted to men who have their own opinions and well-defined boundaries; that is, their own identity.

It's always better to express your differences, and in doing so, show a woman you're confident enough in yourself and your relationship with her that it's ok to disagree. It's this confidence that'll help draw her to you. Ultimately, women want men who stand up for what they believe in despite others' opposing opinions. **She wants you to be your own man.**

So:

👍 Have opinions.

👍 Have preferences.

👍 Have likes and dislikes.

👍 Have an identity.

Here's an example of a guy who's confident enough to express his likes and dislikes:

SALLY: *"Hey, Steve - oh, man, I hate this song! The Barenaked Ladies are so terrible!"*

BRAD: *"What? You're crazy, these guys are so awesome! I love '80s music. Maybe you're too young to appreciate them? Haha. I also love Run DMC."*

SALLY: *"Hahaha, that's terrible!"*

BRAD: *"Hahaha. I'm starving! How does Dairy Queen sound? They make the greatest burgers of all the fast food chains. I hate MacDonald's burgers! Just terrible!"*

SALLY: *"Ya, as far as fast food is concerned, McDicks is terrible! I don't think I've ever had a Dairy Queen burger actually."*

BRAD: *"Fantastic. Let's go. They also have a surprise there
I think you're gonna love!"*

Expressing our opinions is important in demonstrating self-confidence, but how about expressing more serious personal boundaries?

Our personal boundaries help others determine how we expect
to be treated.

"Don't call me after midnight."

"Don't hit me!"

"Don't look through my private things."

Our boundaries are meant to prevent people from taking advantage of us. Have you ever seen a dude who really seems to have
his act together until he falls in love with a beautiful woman and
lets her walk all over him?

People learn to respect you or not depending on how well-defined your boundaries are.

Your job is to communicate these boundaries to others as clearly
and as soon as you can.

Don't let people insult, injure, or do harm to you or your prop-
erty.

Don't let women manipulate or use you.

Here are some simple examples of things women might do or say
that test your boundaries:

"Hey, buy me a drink."

She walks into your place for the first time and starts going through your things.

"I hate guys with long hair... you're gonna have to cut that short!"

She shows up 40 minutes late for a second date without apology or explanation.

"Hey, don't be a fucking idiot!"

"I don't want you going out with those guys any more – they're a bad influence on you!"

These examples are tests that women often throw at you simply because they need to know who you are or where your boundaries are. Children do this with their parents all the time. It's about seeing what they can get away with before mom and dad have reached their limit.

The more you define your expectations and your boundaries, the more confident and secure others will be around you. This is why children ultimately respect parents with clear boundaries. The same is true with adult relationships. A woman needs you to have definable boundaries to respect you and feel comfortable and secure with you.

A boundary has no use if it's not enforced.

Here are boundary-setting responses to each of the above "tests":

HER: *"Hey, buy me a drink."*
RESPONSE: *"Oh, man, you're so right, I love free drinks. So check this out...blah blah blah"*

HER: *She walks into your place for the first time and starts going through your things.*
RESPONSE: *"Hey, don't be so nosey, Mrs. Posey."*

HER: *"I hate guys with long hair… you're gonna have to cut that short!"*
RESPONSE: *"Well, only because you're so hot!" Then let your hair grow longer and add a magnificent beard to your repertoire.*

HER: *She shows up 40 minutes late for a second date without apology or explanation.*
RESPONSE: *Either don't make a third date or leave before she arrives.*

HER: *"Hey, don't be a fucking idiot!"*
RESPONSE: *"Haha, you're so right, I'm sooo stupid. See ya."*

HER: *"I don't want you going out with those guys any more – they're a bad influence on you!"*
RESPONSE: *"Nah, they're decent guys, but I do appreciate that you care."*

When you stop people from stepping over your boundaries, you're inviting them to respect you.

People don't have to agree with you to respect you.

Remember, being comfortable expressing your opinions and clarifying your personal boundaries (especially when they have been crossed) actually makes you attractive to women. By contrast, you'll scare women away if you're overly-agreeable and don't have firm personal boundaries you readily defend.

SCORE RESISTANCE

Women want a nice guy with a spine.

What do women like about the bad boy? His resistance to her—
she can't just have him.
Why is this attractive? Because there can be no attraction without resistance.

> *"There is no power without resistance. Power needs*
> *resistance not only to be powerful, but if it is going to exist*
> *at all. Without resistance, power has no force. It is a blow*
> *against empty air, a fierce punch into darkness that meets*
> *no opposition. So power manufactures its own resistance,*
> *creates its own opponent." ~ Blogger RMJ*

Women simply won't value a guy they can get easily.

If you resist a woman, she will want you more; your value will go
up in her eyes.

What does this resistance look like?

> *Teasing Her – "Your purse is like a horse saddle! Ha ha."*

> *Playfully pretending that she's not your type while also flirt-*
> *ing with her because she is your type. "You're sooo cute! If*
> *you were two inches shorter you'd totally be my type!"*

> *Not answering all of her direct questions, as if you didn't*
> *actually hear them.*

> *Sometimes letting your eyes wander while she's telling a sto-*
> *ry so that she doesn't always have your complete attention.*
> *You'll notice women do this all the time to men.*

Allowing her to contact you (phone, email, text message, IM) more often than you contact her.

Having her jump through some of your hoops (questions, tests, requests, favours) in order to gain your approval.

Specifically not jumping through her hoops. She might say, "Hey, pick me up tonight at 7." And you might respond with, "I can pick you up at 7:30."

Never qualifying yourself until she's qualified herself first. Allow her the space to show her interest in you before you reciprocate.

In general, playfully sending her mixed signals (push/pull).

RESIST JUMPING THROUGH HER HOOPS.

What are hoops?

These are obstacles a woman wants you to jump through in your attempt to gain her interest. It helps her feel in control. The problem with this is that a woman will have a hard time feeling attracted to someone she feels can control.

Ultimately, a woman wants a man who thinks for himself and is on his own path in life. If you're wasting your time doing everything she asks of you, she will, in turn, have a very difficult time finding you attractive. Read any romance novel and you'll see that the woman is always trying to catch the guy who follows his own rules.

Here are some typical hoops or tests and how to address them:

HOOP: *She asks you questions in an attempt to learn every-*

thing about you.

RESPONSE: *Don't answer all of her questions directly at first; make her earn your answers. Always be playful.*

EXAMPLE:

HER: *"So what kind of car do you drive?"*

YOU: *"Oh, man, I wish I could afford a car. Hahaha, that'd be awesome!"*

HER: *"So how old are you?"*

YOU: *"I'm actually turning 48 this September." (This is only funny if you're obviously a different age.)*

HER: *"So do you date a lot?"*

YOU: *"Today? Some, not a lot."*

HOOP: She requests favours from you.

RESPONSE: *Favours are only for women you're already dating. If you've just met her, make her earn any favours you do for her.*

EXAMPLE:

Her: *"Call me tomorrow and we can set up a coffee date."*

You: *"I can tell you when I'm available now: I'm busy this Wednesday night, and all next weekend, so how does coffee Tuesday night sound? If you don't know right now, you can call me tomorrow and let me know."*

Her: *"Can you buy me a drink?"*

You: *"I only buy my close friends drinks, and I don't really know you yet. Hey, have you ever been to Vancouver? There's this story I have about…"*

Her: *"Can you hold my purse for me? I'm just running to the bathroom."*

You: *"I can watch it for you. Just leave it there."*

Her: *"My back and neck are killing me…can you rub my back for me?"*

You: *"Sure, but you have to promise to rub mine too."*

If a woman doesn't see you as the prize, then you've lost her.

No woman will think of you as a prize if she doesn't have to work at winning you over.

Have you ever seen the television show Lost? On that show, the "bad boy" is Sawyer. He hates everybody and never listens to what anyone tells him; he steals, cheats, lies, and is constantly calling everyone else by nicknames that he finds funny and yet the female viewers find him the most attractive character on the show. He also "gets the girl," possibly because he's the only one who doesn't jump through anyone else's hoops.

http://youtu.be/or_BGsW7Mgg

What you need to do is stop worrying about what *her* expectations are; instead, think about what *your* expectations are.

For some men, this can be a challenge. Ask yourself what it is you're looking for in a woman besides her appearance. If your only preferences are that she has big boobs, you're not trying hard enough.

For example, I prefer women who are funny, who enjoy movies, and who like to read. These are small preferences but very important nonetheless. So I use these preferences when I'm assessing the women I date on compatibility. I "screen" her by asking her about the movies she's seen and the books she's read. If she doesn't read, I automatically disqualify her.

For example, I might say, *"I happen to be a movie buff. I grew up dreaming about making movies and now I'm addicted to them. Tell me one of your favourite movies."*

I also prefer women who can banter with me and who are a lot of fun.

I might say, *"So many of my friends are married and never seem to leave their homes anymore because they've become so dependent on their girlfriend or boyfriend—you know what I mean? I think it's sad. So what do you do for fun?"*

I'm also very creative, with a natural desire to continuously challenge myself and develop my inner strengths. So I might ask her something like, *"So what got you into your career? Do you have a passion for what you do?"*

You might even be a little more direct about testing your compatibility if the mood strikes you; for example, *"Besides being devilishly cute, what three qualities do you feel you have that would make me really want to get to know you better?"*

Asking her direct questions as well as clarifying your preferences will give her an opportunity to qualify herself.

EXAMPLE:

"Wait a minute, how old are you?"

"Oh, I hate smokers. I just can't stand the smell."

"I love the summer sun, too. But there's really nothing like watching a movie cuddled up on my couch after the sun's gone down."

"I love back rubs."

"I like eating; are you a good cook?"

While most men are busy chasing after women, jumping through hoops, and "proving" themselves endlessly, the best approach is to resist doing this and be *particular* about whom *you* date.

A quick way to understand this process is to pay attention to how hot women interact with men and do exactly as they do. Attractive women will assume men want them and will make interested men prove they are worthy.

It's *your* job to invite beautiful women to prove themselves to *you*. If you want a woman who's going to stick around long-term or even just for the night, you *must* make her prove herself. She must feel she's being measured up in some way if you ever want her to see you as a man of value.

✎ **Go Online For Resources & Links For This Section: www.IgnoreAndScore.com/attraction**

✎ **Questions About This Section? Email Me Here: questions@IgnoreAndScore.com**

CORE BEHAVIOR: LEADING

WHAT IS LEADING?

You will succeed in dating if you focus on just two things: your behaviours and the emotions you bring out in women.

Men who are very successful with women and dating focus on the following emotions and behaviours:

EMOTIONS: *Her attraction to you and your rapport as a couple*

BEHAVIOURS: *His leading and escalation behaviours*

I've already discussed the best things to ignore and score when it comes to Attraction, so now let's discuss Leading.

Leading is about taking action.

Why do most men fail to be successful in dating and in life? They don't take action.

If you're struggling to attract amazing women into your life, it's because you don't have or use your own power. You don't have that power because you're constantly giving it away.

Here are some ways you may be giving up your power:

- Putting her on a pedestal

- Forcing her to lead; i.e., asking her to make all of the decisions

- Asking for permission

- Constantly apologizing

- Constantly worrying that you'll upset her

- Seeking her approval, praise, and constant attention.

- Instead of voicing your opinions, going along with her and then seeking your "revenge" through passive aggressive behaviours

- Trying to manipulate her by bragging, lying, or being domineering

How can any woman, especially one with high social value (a woman adored by many men), possibly find you attractive if you're busy giving her all of your power?

The worst thing is that she thinks she wants that power, but ultimately, it will demolish her attraction and respect for you. It's called chronic male supplication, and it's killing the love lives of this generation: Men Supplicating to Women and the Women Who Hate Them for It - my next eBook?)

It's universally understood that women are attracted to leaders. This doesn't mean you need to be a social leader, although it helps; it simply means your behaviours must communicate to her that you're in control of yourself.

She needs to feel that you're able to make decisions, take action, and ignore your own fears. These are leadership behaviours. These are the behaviours that will communicate to her "this guy has his shit together and will not only support and protect me when I need it, he'll lead me into experiences I've never had before."

A woman wants to be with a man who can lead, a man she can trust enough to take over.

Ultimately, women won't be attracted to men who are burdens; in other words, you must manage your own life, home, wealth, health, and passions. If you spend your time asking her to make decisions, she'll worry that you're just a long-term burden. Suggestions for displaying leadership qualities:

- 👍 If she smiles at you, you must go over and introduce yourself.

- 👍 If you have gone through the trouble of walking over and introducing yourself, you must at least try to get her number before you leave.

- 👍 Don't ask her where she wants to go for dinner, simply surprise her.

- 👍 Take her hand when helping her out of a car.

- 👍 Go the long way around a car to get to her door.

- 👍 Guide her safely across a crowded room, either by the hand, or by holding out your arm for her.

- 👍 Walk her safely to her car.

- 👍 Playfully suggest what she should wear before you pick her up.

- 👍 Kiss her on the first date, or at least attempt to, even if it's awkward. If there's a second date, she'll know you'll be trying again, which means she's okay with it, otherwise there wouldn't be a second date.

- 👍 Spend time being more social, even if it means you must leave your comfort zone once in a while—these skills translate into many aspects of your life.

- 👍 Have your own opinions; don't worry about disagreeing sometimes.

- 👍 Have your own personality, identity, and clearly-defined boundaries.

- 👎 Don't fake-laugh.

- 👍 Have self-discipline. This shows up in your ability to stay healthy, save money, plan trips, and ultimately manage your own life.

- 👍 Have a passion independent of women—perhaps a hobby, or your day job. Your enthusiasm for your work will go a long way to winning over most women, no matter what your work actually is.

In fact, both men and women are attracted to leaders.

Why?

Most people would simply prefer to "obey" rather than "follow." There's no risk; there's no responsibility. It's just easier.

If you look at the average man who's terrible with women, you'll see he exhibits this "follower" mindset. He obeys. He puts women on pedestals and worries too much about getting her permission or approval. This is a victim mentality. These same guys say things like "Oh, she wouldn't like me because I don't make enough money."

Luckily, this isn't you.

Victims don't read eBooks about women, sex, and dating. That's a leadership trait.

IGNORE

IGNORE YOUR INSECURITIES

Your success with women is your responsibility. Whatever diffi-
culties have led you down your current path might not be your
fault, but they are your responsibility. No one else is responsible
for your life except you.

I challenge you to start noticing the voices in your head that
come from your insecurities. It's these voices that make you
cocky and boastful in an attempt to persuade others that you're
better than you are, or that make you very meek and shy, as a
means to shield others from discovering the real, unlikable you.

When you hide or demand the attention and approval of others, you're allowing your insecurities to dictate your life. This is
a tragic mistake.

How do insecurities keep us down?

Your insecurities attempt to convince you of things that are not
useful. For example:

🖓 You must have a beautiful girlfriend that will make your
friends jealous.

🖓 If this beautiful woman rejects you, it will only confirm

that you're really just an idiot.

🖓 You are who your friends think you are.

🖓 You must look, dress, and act the part.

🖓 Your car is your status.

🖓 Your income is your status; your financial success is your power.

🖓 Your ability to attract women dictates how others will see and judge you.

🖓 Your physical appearance is who you are.

🖓 Your powerful friends define you.

🖓 You must be well-liked to succeed in life.

🖓 It doesn't matter who you are in private, it only matters who you are in the eyes of others.

Not one of the above statements is true. They're simply aspects of how we define ourselves. We often determine our personal value based upon the approval and definitions of others. If we're desperate for our friends to be jealous of the women we date, we've completely lost the importance of relationships and why we seek them out.

Women are not tools for social success. Dating is not meant to be only about shallow, personal gain.

The truth is there is no real consequence to social judgments. Our survival-mode egos drive us to seek social approval based upon criteria others have made up.

Marketers overwhelm our everyday lives with campaigns and advertising to remind us how we're not quite good enough until we own this or that product or we buy into one more service. We're constantly reminded of what we lack.

This is one of the many reasons a lot of men feel lost and inadequate with women. We're socially conditioned to believe we are essentially inadequate if we lack certain qualities, social status, or possessions. If we allow ourselves to believe this, we will never be happy because our identity will always be tied up in something external beyond our ultimate control.

For example, if I am a BMW owner and believe BMW ownership brings with it great social proof and approval, my perception of self-worth becomes contingent on having that car. If something happens that I lose my car or a better car comes on the market, my self-worth is undermined.

I've found that the voices in my head that are encouraging, positive, and empowering are the voices I listen to the most now. I've gradually learned to ignore the voices in my head that are actively challenging me to seek the approval of others before I can be happy with myself.

Any thoughts you have that undermine your self-approval are to be questioned. Self-love takes practice!

How do you think the world's greatest pickup artists become so good? Through perseverance, careful introspection, and continuous self-improvement, they learned to become the kind of men women naturally respond to. These same guys were willing to be publicly rejected over and over again so they could learn what it takes to succeed.

We fear that if we're rejected, we're not good enough. This is nonsense.

As we discussed earlier, everyone has his or her own reasons for liking or disliking others; those reasons have very little to do with you. A woman who would normally love you might turn you down on the day that you meet her simply because of the mood she's in.

In reality, a woman's disinterest in you is simply unfortunate; it should not be over-dramatized beyond simple inopportunity. Learn to ignore negative thoughts that prevent you from moving forward and finding success.

IGNORE YOUR FRIENDS AND FAMILY

You can't choose your family, and you will always be stuck with them. This fact will never change. What you can change is family's negative influence on your dating life.

If your parents had a dysfunctional relationship when you were growing up, you've probably learned unhealthy relationship behaviours. Don't repeat the mistakes of your parents in your own relationships.

Often we feel pressured by mom and dad to "find a nice girl and get married" so they can have grand kids. Obviously, this added pressure isn't going to help anyone.

You must learn to disassociate from family pressures. There is a huge difference between loving and respecting your parents and doing everything they say. Now that you're an adult, your parents no longer have any say about what you do, who you are, or how you behave.

Let them have their opinions, but don't ever let them dictate your life! Do as you please. Learn to act without their permission and approval.

Many of us become trapped in an ongoing parent–child relationship and never learn to speak with our own voice. This is something you must do if you're to expect future success with women. Another problem is that mothers raise their boys to avoid challenges and risk and to otherwise become more feminized. This is a tragic mistake for men. We can't just blame mom though, because she's simply doing her best.

How many of us had absent fathers? Either he wasn't around or, if he was around, he wasn't really "available." This has caused many men to become confused about what it means to be manly, assertive, strong, consistent, bold, powerful, courageous, and dominant.

Therefore, men like you and me, who read eBooks like this one, are the few who've decided to step beyond the shortcomings of our upbringing in our attempt to clear a brand new path for ourselves.

Learn to be self-directed, motivated, proud, honest, curious, and adventurous. Maturity is the stage where you're able to make choices for yourself, based on your own inner-direction.

Now is the time to start ignoring the bad advice your friends and family are giving you and seek the insights of men who really know what they're doing.

Getting advice from women is a mistake because they don't understand dating from a male perspective.

Getting advice from your friends who haven't dated since the late '80s or who've been married for 20 years is also a mistake.

You wouldn't go to the local unemployment line when seeking advice on investing your money, so why seek dating advice from people who don't truly understand the dynamics of human seduction?

There are plenty of books written by real experts on dating; go read them and take the time to trust your own inner voice.

IGNORE YOUR PAST DATING MISTAKES

We base our beliefs largely on our own experiences. This is a mistake because if you've never had a lot of success in the past, you'll never have reason to believe it's possible in the future. It's the chicken and egg problem: What comes first—confidence or experience?

Take some time to learn from your past experiences; then let them go.

DID YOU DO STUPID THINGS THAT DROVE HER AWAY? *Don't repeat them.*

DID YOU PICK UP A GIRL AT THE BAR WHO ENDED UP STEALING YOUR CELL PHONE AND YOUR ROOMMATE'S CAMERA? *(Vegas?) Be more cautious.*

DID YOU DATE A GIRL WHO ENDED UP BEING MARRIED? *What were the warning signs you ignored?*

DID YOU DATE A GIRL WHO ENDED UP BEING A STALKER? *What red flags did you ignore?*

WHAT WOMEN HAVE YOU MET THAT REALLY FLOORED YOU AND THEN GOT AWAY? *What drew them to you to begin with?*

Ex-girlfriends can become anchors that only pull you down. You've likely already spent plenty of time mulling over your missteps; now it's time to move on. If you're thinking of past girl-friends, it should only be because you feel proud of these past experiences.

It's the guys who continue to re-live their past relationships who are the most nervous meeting new women. When you're stuck in the past, you'll always be dead last.

When it comes to ex-girlfriends, you shouldn't settle for "let's just be friends" so that you can orbit her life, like a moth around a flame, with the secret hope you can still get her back. This is a waste of energy and focus. As you sit around thinking of her, hoping she'll come back to you, she's out with friends getting laid. Stop sulking and start acting.

Your past girlfriends are in your past for a reason.

Learn about the attitudes you had that worked best for attracting women to you in the past; how did you act, talk, and walk that drew her to you? Then reuse these same behaviours. Remember how cocky and funny you were when you met Melissa? Remember how brave you were when you walked over to that table of girls, and how you ended up dating Sandra?

IGNORE YOUR FEARS

Obviously, if you had no fears, you would automatically have more success with women, right?

Wrong.

It's not fear that causes guys to fail with women; it's a lack of courage. Fear is actually our friend because it warns us that something's going to happen that we're not prepared for. Danger Will Robinson! Danger!

The number one thing women say they want in a man who approaches them is confidence, but what's just as necessary is sincerity.

If you're nervous, but you want to meet a woman because you're curious about her and attracted to her, she'll see it in your face and read it in your body language.

Any woman will feel some sympathy for you if you're nervous, but she'll be attracted to the fact that you were courageous enough to approach her in the first place.

Courage is taking action in spite of our fears. It's courage that attracts women, not lack of fear.

Here's why.

As we know, attraction is tension. Without tension, there can be no attraction; without attraction, there can be no first date. Fear automatically builds tension. Therefore, if you approach a girl and you're nervous and worried, you're given the golden opportunity to do two things: build tension (she'll feel that you're nervous even if you hardly show it) and show her you're courageous (she sees you're chatting with her even though you're nervous). This approach will go a long way toward building attraction between you and her.

If you go up to a woman to chat and have absolutely no nervousness, she might have no emotional reaction towards you at all, leaving her confused about whether you were hitting on her or not.

Of course, if you act goofy, creepy, or even potentially dangerous, then you'll change the good tension into bad tension. Her attraction will quickly shift to repulsion or fear.

This is why having fear is a good thing but only so far as it helps you prepare and communicate your interest. Ultimately, you must learn to act despite your fears to be courageous and attractive.

When talking with women, use your fear to build tension and lure them with your sincerity.

Which of the following opening lines do you think will resonate more with a woman you've just met?

"Hi, my name's Robert. I think you are so beautiful."

Or

"Hi, my name's Robert. Ha, wow, suddenly I'm so nervous. I haven't met a girl who can make nervous in a really long time. So what's your name?"

In reality, either approach can work just fine. The key to the second opening line is that you're willing to honestly express that you're nervous. It works better, only if you're being completely sincere, because it shows her you're willing to be honest while also being courageous.

It is a mistake, however, to keep referring to your nervousness or use other self-deprecating remarks. Say it once then never bring it up again. Saying it the one time is a way for you to settle your nerves a little; honesty can loosen the tension in your body.

SCORE

SCORE YOUR OWN APPROVAL

Seeking the approval of others is the fastest way to repulse the women you meet. As we've discussed, this is because women don't want to date a man who's a burden. When you seek her approval, you leave her no room to respect you.

Examples of approval-seeking behaviours:

- Do you worry about sharing your opinions with others for fear they'll disagree?

- Do you worry about what you're wearing because you're not sure what others will think?

- Do you have trouble making decisions about things without the advice of others?

- Do you have trouble listening to others because you're too worried about what you're going to say next?

- Do you worry about how you look?

- Do you brag about yourself whenever you can?

- Do you judge others harshly?

🖓 Do you only go after girls that other guys have already shown interest in?

🖓 Do you prefer buying trendy clothes so as to fit in instead of buying clothes that fit you well?

🖓 Do you behave in certain ways to impress others? (e.g., going to the gym excessively.)

🖓 Do you have trouble saying no?

The only way to grow past our fears of social rejection is to reinforce our own self-esteem.

It's up to you to be okay with you.

If the only opinion that matters is your own, you can choose to be pleased with yourself each and every day despite what others may think of you.

This means learning to ignore other people's negative and positive evaluations of you. You need to trust your own sense of self-worth. If you rely on good evaluations of yourself from others for your self-esteem, you'll just as easily be persuaded by their bad opinions of you.

STOP JUDGING YOURSELF AND OTHERS

No woman is ever going to open up to you if she feels you might wound her by judging her. Like us, women want to protect themselves, and if you spend your time judging her, she'll never open up.

> *"If you judge people, you have no time to love them."*
> ~ Mother Teresa

Do you spend your time at the office gossiping about others? When you gossip, you demonstrate to others that you can't be trusted.

Be aware of your internal dialogue.

The easiest way to quiet the inner judge is to always do your best, keeping in mind that your best depends on your health, mood, and abilities at any given time or circumstance. If you always do everything the best you can, your inner judge will have no reason to criticize you. You'll discover that your quieted inner critic will slowly cease to cause you stress and doubt.

When you're done judging yourself and others, you'll have an amazing amount of energy left for self-approval, trust, and love.

Go Online For Resources & Links For This Section: www.IgnoreAndScore.com/Leading

Questions About This Section? Email Me Here: questions@IgnoreAndScore.com

KEEP HER: RAPPORT & ESCALATION

ABOUT THIS SECTION

Here's a scenario: You've met a girl, and you're interested in seeing her more. You're attracted to each other, and you're having fun. Now it's time to change the dynamic to the next stage of rapport; how you get there is called escalation. The second half of this eBook is about escalating first contact into something more comfortable and intimate.

CORE EMOTION: RAPPORT

WHAT IS RAPPORT?

Rapport is the stage of dating that comes after attraction has been established. If she's not attracted to you, any rapport you build will lead you to the dreaded "let's be friends" zone. This is a tough prison to escape from, so I suggest that if you don't have a handle on attraction, go back and review the first half of this eBook.

Let's continue.

Have you ever met someone you really connected with? It felt like you had known them for years, right?

This is called *rapport*.

Rapport is trust, intimacy, and shared understanding. We are drawn to these types of connections because they feel familiar and safe, like being home.

Why does rapport matter with women and dating? It matters because attraction isn't enough. Dating is bonding. We date so that we can get to know another person. It's what many women will call "connection." If a woman doesn't feel there is any type of connection, no matter how attractive you are, she'll move on. Rapport is the connection of mutual understanding. It's like rowing a boat with another person: when you're in sync, your boat will move forward; if you row out of sync, your boat falters and goes nowhere.

What does rapport look like on a date?

When two people are in rapport, they'll unconsciously begin to mimic each other's movements, expressions, breathing, tone of voice, and even emotions. This is called *mirroring*. It's true that our emotions are contagious because the more rapport we have with someone, the more likely we are to mirror them.

If you sit quietly and watch a couple who are either happily married or who have just fallen in love, you'll notice that they will copy each other. If one scratches his face, the other will too. If one crosses her legs, the other will too. If one leans in, the other will follow. It's completely unconscious and pretty amazing to see.

As you become aware of this mirroring behaviour in yourself and others, you can use it to your advantage. If you mirror a person's behaviours, she will generally be friendlier to you. Mirroring is subtle; if you exaggerate, it may come across as if you're mocking the person you're mirroring.

This can be a powerful tool when on a date where you feel there is no chemistry. If you're attractive (see the first part of this eBook), she'll want to create rapport with you and she'll naturally start to mirror you. She'll want to play less and have deeper conversations.

Your exchanges should be fun and flirty at first, and then, when the time is right, your interactions should become more serious, intense, and meaningful.

How does having rapport help us when dating?

- 👍 Rapport assumes a level of shared views and relatedness; we seek this common ground with those we are attracted to.

- 👍 We want to trust those we date, and when we have rapport with someone, there is an implied level of trust.

- 👍 Rapport helps us to feel seen, heard, and understood.

- 👍 If we have rapport with someone on many levels, we're more likely to share belief systems and moral structures.

- 👍 Before a woman will allow herself to become vulnerable for sexual intimacy, she must first deeply trust that you will not hurt her; rapport helps imply this level of trust and comfort.

WHEN IS THE RIGHT TIME TO BUILD RAP-PORT?

Rapport comes after attraction.

Timing is an important part of building rapport. You'll fail if you attempt to build rapport with a woman when she's not yet attracted to you because you haven't established a basis for deepening intimacy. Or you'll turn her into a friend and lose the possibility of intimacy.

It's your job to continue to tease and flirt while seeking evidence of her interest. In the pickup community, these are called Indicators of Interest (IOIs).

A major problem with dating is that women tend to be very subtle about their interest while men tend to be too obvious. Learn to communicate your interest more subtly. The world of subtle communication is all about body language and innuendos. A woman's interest will rarely be direct. Therefore, you must pay attention to her indirect signs.

How does the average guy show his interest? Compliments, strong eye contact, and flirting. Men express their interest in a masculine way: we're more direct. It's our job to take a risk, approach, flirt, and lead.

How does a woman show her interest? Women are more passive when it comes to dating; therefore, they act differently. If she's interested in you, she'll let you know, so pay attention. She'll do her best to be approachable and beautiful. Her body language will open up to you: she'll lean into you; she'll touch you more, and she'll laugh at your silly jokes.

Basically, when she's attracted to you, she'll start trying to build rapport with you.

Watch for the following behaviours:

   She teases you – *"Oh my, your hands are as small as mine! He he he."*

   Her body turns to face you more.

   She leans slightly into you as if she's trying to listen closer.

   Her eyes dilate—it's called puppy dog eyes.

   She laughs too much at your lame jokes.

👍 She touches you; even punching and playful pushing counts.

👍 She becomes overly agreeable: *"I love that song, too!"*

👍 She starts asking personal questions about you: *"So, what do you do for a living?"*

👍 She makes more eye contact with you because she's suddenly more curious about you.

👍 She tries to find commonalities.

These are all indicators that she's attracted to you and wants to know you more. This is evidence that it's time to transition gradually to rapport.

HOW DO WE BUILD RAPPORT?

Once she has demonstrated IOIs, it's time to build rapport with her. In building rapport, you need to use the four following skills:

Listening and demonstrating sincerity, trustworthiness, and curiosity.

Being Sincere and Honest: If she suspects you're being fake, sarcastic, or phony, she'll close off any possibility of rapport. Being honest is one of the fastest ways of showing your sincerity. This might mean you confess something you normally wouldn't, like "I shouldn't tell you this, but you actually make me nervous. It's so strange." Just be sure that when you say things, you really do mean them; a woman knows when you're being insincere.

Being Trustworthy: Rapport is all about trust. The more you can demonstrate your trustworthiness, the more a woman will be willing to open up to you. You build her trust by first trusting her. Try sharing a secret or a story you normally wouldn't tell. This might invite her to do the same. You should also not share the secrets of others with her because she'll see that you're likely to share her secrets with others. Basically, it's best not to gossip about others at all.

Being Curious: When you're interested and curious about someone, it comes across in your face and what you say and how you say it. When you show you're curious about a woman, she'll enjoy the attention and energy.

Being a Good Listener: When you allow someone the space to completely be free and un-judged, they'll open up to you very quickly. I can't tell you how many times I've heard a woman say something like, "I can't believe I'm telling you this right now!"

Be careful not to be openly opinionated about the faults of others. If she hears you judging others for their faults or gossiping about your close friends, she'll quickly learn you're not the type of person she's safe opening up to.

Sharing commonalities is rapport:

- Fashion sense and style – This is why Goth guys date Goth chicks, for example.

- Speaking the same language – Perhaps you can both speak sign language?

- Using the same vocabulary – Street slang, types of words and phrases, etc.

- Hobbies, interests, and passions – From making model airplanes to reading the same books.

- Music, books, and television shows – Liking the same movies helps when choosing one to see.

- Religious beliefs and faith systems.

- Cultural backgrounds.

- Taste in food and drinks – Perhaps you're both vegetarians.

- Career, income levels, and social influence – Perhaps you're both highly social and active in the community.

- Love for pets and animals.

- Champions for fundraisers and local charities.

- Life styles – You both may be introverts, for example.

CONNECT THROUGH STORYTELLING

Why storytelling?

Storytelling is a unique way to engage your listener emotionally in a way that regular conversation simply can't. A good story quickly conveys your values, your passions, and your personality.

If you think about your most charismatic friends, you'll realize they are compelling, entertaining storytellers; they can tell a story about anything and make it interesting. Good storytelling is a skill that takes practice.

Learn how to tell a story, and you'll seduce any woman you meet.

Here are some quick tips on storytelling:

👍 **BE EXPRESSIVE.** Powerful storytelling isn't about what you're saying; it's about how you're saying it. Ask yourself this: If someone listening to your story doesn't speak your language, will they be curious about what you're saying, or will they immediately lose interest? The surest way to be expressive is to be emotionally involved in a story. Use your hands; change the volume of your voice; and use your body. It's better to be over the top than boring.

👍 **KEEP IT PERSONAL.** The more personal you can make your stories, the more likely a woman is to reciprocate. The emotional impact of a story can have incredible impact on how connected you feel to each other. Telling stories that don't have emotional resonance for you will have little emotional impact on her.

👎 **DON'T JUST TELL A STORY, ENGAGE YOUR AUDIENCE.** Your job isn't to be a clown who entertains a girl on a date; your job is to express who you are and to find out who she is. If you're just talking to fill space, she'll get bored. Involve her in a story; let her speak too. If she's involved, she'll relate better to the story.

Tell stories that convey your value, without bragging. There's a difference between a story that ends with you explaining how cool your new car is and a story that briefly mentions the car while you rushed your dog to the veterinarian. Let your stories hint upon how interesting your life is, without making your stories a reason to brag and feel good about yourself. She'll know you're bragging, and you'll come across as a douche.

Pay attention to how popular standup comics tell stories. These guys spend their whole lives learning how to tell an engaging story. Pay attention.

HAVE A POINT.   If you waste five minutes telling a story that has no tension, conflict, or outcome, or you jump around too much, you'll have told her that you're a boring man whom she should avoid. Make sure your story goes somewhere.

KEEP IT SHORT.   You can tell if your story is going on too long when she's looking around the room with a bored look on her face. Cut out any information in your story that doesn't help get you to the punch line.

KEEP IT FUN.   Not every story needs to be about the secrets grandpapa told you before he died. Remember that she'll associate any emotions she feels from your stories with you. If your stories are endlessly sad and morose, you'll be pushing her away. Keep the stories uplifting whenever you can.

IGNORE

UNDERSTAND AND ALLAY HER RESISTANCE

Women fear the very real dangers of physical violence, emotional trauma, and even social judgment when meeting and dating men.

Most men are much bigger and stronger than most women, which is something we men often take for granted. We don't think about this obvious danger when dating, but women do. As such, a woman will rely on certain social barriers to keep a man at a safe distance until she's interested and comfortable.

If you're acting overly nervous, aggressive in a domineering way, or just creepy (e.g., you don't smile much), you're likely to set off her internal alarm bell to stay away from you. Once this alarm goes off, you're far from any chance of getting the girl.

If you're scaring women away, you need to step back and investigate your own behaviours. Question yourself about which of her boundaries you may have over-stepped and what body language you were expressing that pushed her away.

Women also fear social judgment.

Historically, it was men of government and church who dictated the rules of sexual propriety for women; open sexual expression was strictly discouraged, especially for women. This is why we have so many foul words for women who enjoy having sex, but very few for men.

Women might be called sluts, whores, skanks, or easy, yet men who sleep around are actually viewed in a positive light.

Most women feel a very real and understandable need to not be socially stigmatized. This is why most women will not flaunt their sexual adventures for fear of being judged or labeled a slut.

This is why most women won't openly approach you at the bar or brag about going home with some random guy; yet many men will as if it's a badge of honour.

A woman's resistance to you has everything to do with her own well-being. It's a cop-out to blame a woman for being a cock-tease because of your inability to attract her and make her feel comfortable with you.

Let's learn how to recognize this kind of resistance and how to overcome it.

What does her resistance look like?

Her resistance could look like many things. Basically, a woman can block your sexual advances at any stage of the game, from getting her name to getting her panties off. It's different for every woman and will always depend upon how comfortable you help her feel.

Some women love attention so much that they'll flirt with you for hours while enjoying your compliments and obvious interest, but as soon as you try to get a phone number, she'll shoot you down.

Other women might go all the way to the bedroom with you only to suddenly put the brakes on when you're trying to get her bra off. All women are different and have varying levels of resistance to a man's advances.

REMOVING HER RESISTANCE

You can remove a woman's resistance if she is attracted to you and if you have developed rapport with her; in fact, a woman will do pretty much anything you want if she's attracted to you and you feel familiar to her.

You can help allay her resistance by creating a compelling, comfortable, and safe sexual environment—emphasis on sexual.

Obviously, she's going to feel completely safe with you if she thinks you're gay or have no interest in her, which is how many men end up being "just a friend."   As you are subtly ensuring her of her safety, always maintain sexual tension in your interactions to avoid becoming just a friend.

You can provide a safe, erotic environment.

Follow these simple rules, and you'll naturally remove her fears and resistance:

   👍 Be honest with her – about everything.

   👍 Always be escalating, even if it's more gradual.

   👍 Build anticipation and comfort with a push/pull dynamic.

Be honest with her – about everything.

When a woman trusts you, she'll open herself up to you. It's simple.

Many men will lie in order to help a woman relax and open up. However, this rarely works for long. Keeping up with your tangled web of lies can be an arduous task and prevents you from acting natural; a woman will sense your insincerity and be scared away.

Instead, being completely honest surprises women and naturally draws them to you.

When a woman asks you something you might normally want to lie about but you don't, she'll be completely amazed. It's really something you have to experience to appreciate.

For example, have you ever been asked how old you are by a woman who's obviously far younger than you are? I can still recall talking with a young woman who looked about eighteen or nineteen when, halfway through our chat, she said, "So, how old are you?" to which I replied "I'm 30. Hey, check out that guy's tie! Ha ha ha...."

Her initial response was "Wow, you're 30? You do know I'm nineteen, right?" to which I replied "Holy crap!? What? Wow... I'm sorry. I totally thought you were 16. You're way too old for me." Then I hip-checked her in fun. She laughed and the age issue never came up again.

If a woman brings up a topic you suspect she's worried about, it's sometimes best to show her how you're not worried about it, which might lead her to feel the same way.

Another good one is "Are you dating anyone else?" I used to think I needed to hide the other women I was dating because I assumed all women would hate the idea of dating me if I was dating someone else. But I soon learned that women prefer your honesty so that they can decide for themselves if they'll continue seeing you.

When you're honest, even when she doesn't really want to hear what you have to say, she'll automatically respect you for saying it.

Always be escalating.

Resistance isn't rejection.

It took me years to understand this, so pay attention.

If you're dating a woman, and you're trying to escalate from one stage to the next (let's say you're going in for the first kiss) and she stops you, or she gives you the cheek, it doesn't mean you've lost all the ground you made up to get to that stage.

Her resistance isn't her saying *no* – she's simply saying *not* yet.

If she turns down your kiss, it's just a sign she's not ready to kiss you. It doesn't mean you're starting all over from the first step; it simply means you need to build up her tension, attraction, interest, and comfort.

The less you react negatively to her resistance, the more she'll learn to trust and appreciate you. Don't be that guy who becomes completely withdrawn and pouty simply because she's pushed you away a little. Her resistance is integral to your success.

Just remember that you must always be escalating.

If she stopped you from the first kiss on your first date, attempt to kiss her again on the next date.

If she wasn't comfortable having sex with you on date three or four, you must attempt on dates five or six.

A woman may not be comfortable enough to have sex with you by the third date, but she'll be greatly disappointed if you don't even try. You'll actually do more damage to the relationship if you don't even try to escalate than if you do but she resists your advances.

It's her job to resist you, and it's your job to always be escalating. If she continues to show interest (setting another date, for example), think of her resistance as a speed bump not a stop sign.

PUSH/PULL DYNAMIC

The push/pull dynamic is about pumping up her anticipation. You should be taking two steps forward for every one step back. It's this step back that helps her acclimatize to your new escalating behaviours. If you don't take that one step back, you'll likely overwhelm her with your escalation.

For example, you might touch her lower arm, then her upper arm, then stop. Then you might touch her upper arm, then her lower back, then stop. Then you might touch her lower back, then hold her hand, then stop.

Two steps forward, one step back. This approach allows her time to feel comfortable with each level of escalation you introduce.

If you tried going from holding her hand to kissing her to grabbing her ass, you're not giving her any time to feel comfortable with each stage of intimacy.

This is one reason you'll hear the advice "never have sex on the first date," because otherwise she may feel buyer's remorse. Women have a tendency to feel slutty if they feel like they've rushed into bed with a guy, which means she might not call you back out of embarrassment even if she really liked you.

When you pay attention to her body language, you'll know when she's ready to be kissed, hugged, and touched and when you should step back to give her space.

Don't be that guy who's completely unaware of a woman's apprehension. Sometimes men will approach a woman at a bar but stand completely in her physical and personal space while facing her directly. This is a very challenging and threatening posture and will spook most women away.

When you pay attention to a woman's physical response to your presence, you'll know when you need to give her more space or when not to face her so directly so that she feels no physical threat from you.

If you're going in for a kiss and she pulls away, it's your job to respond in a non-judgmental, easy-going way. If you react poorly—e.g., you become angry or pouty—you'll only communicate to her that you're immature and completely out of control of your own emotions.

Always be composed.

Don't allow unexpected resistance to foul your mood or disrupt your flow. When you're non-reactive to her resistance (almost like you're aware of it but you're ignoring it), she'll automatically feel more comfortable with you.

Allow her to resist you at her own leisure, without it upsetting your composure. When you feel it's the right time to kiss her, then simply do it. She'll either accept it or not.

Little things upset insecure people; don't be insecure: Resistance isn't rejection.

IGNORE YOUR JEALOUSY AND LEARN FROM IT

As you become more successful at meeting and attracting women of higher and higher quality, you'll start to realize that the hotter your dates get, the more men they have in their lives. I can't tell you how often I've heard women say, "I have more guy friends than women friends because I get along better with guys. Women can be sooo catty."

I figured these women didn't realize that most of their guy friends would sleep with them at the drop of a hat. Knowing this only helped fuel my insecurities and any hidden jealousy I may have felt about it.

I've since learned that feelings of jealousy are good for two things: Warning you that your girlfriend has other options besides you and that being jealous is a great way to push her away.

The basic truth is that other men will always want to sleep with your girlfriend. Some of these guys will be orbiters (men who befriend her while secretly wanting to catch her) and others will just be friends. Some of the men in her life will actually be ex-boyfriends or ex-lovers.

What can you do to prevent yourself from being jealous every time you see your girlfriend chatting with the good-looking hunk from the office, or because her ex-boyfriend is still in her life?

    👆 Don't date girls who need constant attention from other guys.

Some women simply need constant attention from men and will always be needy and flirty. These girls tend to be younger than 30 and like to have a lot of fun. If you're struggling to control your jealousy, don't date these types of women. There are plenty of woman who prefer only the attention of their boyfriend.

👍 Pay attention to why you are feeling jealous.

Be honest with yourself whenever you feel jealous. Ask yourself if you're being jealous because she's really being inappropriate or if you're simply a jealous guy. If you're being jealous simply because you're insecure, you must work on yourself instead of on her. Ask yourself if you're always jealous or only jealous with this one woman.

👍 Realize that jealousy is a type of fear.

As you date more and more women, you'll realize that jealousy is really just your fear of losing someone you like. As you age from your 20s to your 30s, you'll naturally find you're less and less jealous. This is because most of our fears are driven from a "scarcity mentality" that we hold onto from our youth. We fear losing a particular woman because we think she's one-of-a-kind.

Great women are far more common than we think. As you age and date more, you'll realize that if one woman wants to cheat on you, it doesn't matter, because there are a million more great women who won't.

The truth is that most women have no interest in cheating on their boyfriends, especially women who are happy in their relationships.

Choose wisely.

👍 Develop clear communication of your boundaries with your love interest.

If she doesn't know which behaviours of hers upset you, she'll never have the opportunity to change them or to explain herself so that you're less distressed when she behaves a certain way. Perhaps she hangs out with that dude you hardly know or perhaps she's flirty with guys because she doesn't realize it upsets you. Who knows? Why spend time guessing what her motives are when you can simply ask her about it yourself. Make sure that when you bring up your insecurities you do it confidently and with care. Being an overbearing, jealous boyfriend will ultimately push your girlfriend away.

> Jealousy may be a symptom of a bigger problem: your control issues.

If you think you can control every aspect of your girlfriend's life, you should seek professional help. Asking for the advice of a counselor is a very positive way to grow as a man. Wanting or needing to control someone is neurotic, unacceptable, and a guaranteed way to always feel helpless and angry.

> Trust grows with time and experience and helps ease feelings of jealousy.

The reality is that if you trust someone completely, you'll never worry about them cheating on you, no matter who they interact with. This deep level of trust comes from a number of places: experience, self-confidence, and the more profound understanding that it's better to sometimes be cheated on than it is to never trust.

The best advice I can give you is this: Never let her see you acting jealous. If you're unsure of something she's doing, simply ask for clarification as casually as you can: "Wait a minute, babe... who's this John character you're having lunch with... I've never heard you speak of him."

Never become angry because you feel jealous. Doing so will erode her attraction for you and reinforce immature behaviours you might still be holding onto since middle school.

IGNORE HER TESTS

So how does a woman get comfortable with you? She tests you. It's a woman's job for her own well-being to make sure you're not lying, cheating, or pretending to be someone you're not.

The funny thing is that women will test you from the moment they meet you and for the rest of your shared relationship; they'll test you often without realizing they're doing it. You may not realize it either, to the detriment of your relationship.

How do women test you?

Tests vary for every woman. The more insecure she is, the more she'll test you. This is one reason I prefer to date highly evolved, self-realized, and independent women. They rarely need to test because they rarely feel the need for the security such tests may bring.

When you first meet a woman, she might test you to see how you'll react to certain questions or behaviours.

Some women will ask pointed questions to see if you'll squirm or lie: *"How old are you?" "Is your girlfriend hot?" "How many women have you ever slept with?"* The right answer is to either ignore the question or to tease her in turn: *"I'm old enough to know not to answer that question," "Oh wow, she's sooo hot! She reminds me of mom,"* and *"Today? Some, not a lot."*

Some women will whine and complain. A woman will always respond more positively to you if you refuse to play along with these negative behaviours. You might respond with *"I'm not going to listen to this whining anymore."*

Some women might start flirting with other men in front of you to see how you'll deal with it. You can either walk away, showing her you're not interested in playing games, or you can call her out on her behaviour: *"I think you're a great girl, but I have no interest in playing silly games or fighting for your attention. If you want to flirt with these boys, go ahead, but I'm out of here."* Remember to speak with a calm, confident voice; don't be whiny. Maintain your composure at all times.

As time progresses, her tests may change according to her insecurities.

She might flip out over nothing, causing an emotional scene. If, at any time, her behaviour is irrational and overly dramatic, it's not your job to just take it. Remaining composed is important, but it doesn't mean you must endure any abusive behaviour. Explain that she must respect you as you respect her and walk away if need be.

Your job, if you really like this woman, is to address her insecurities while never acting insecurely yourself. If she flips out on you because you showed up five minutes late, stay composed; explain to her that her over-the-top behaviour is uncalled-for. It's even best to walk away from such a scene, allowing her time to regain her composure.

How do you pass her tests?

Stay composed.

This means you're always calm, especially when she's not. This means you walk away from any abusive behaviour. Sometimes women do things just to see how you'll react. Ignoring her doesn't work, but ignoring her tests will.

Ultimately, she wants to see that you're reliable. She wants to feel that you'll always have your wits about you no matter how dire the circumstances. She needs to feel assured you're stable and know your own mind.

This is exactly why you must never become upset or unsettled by her tests. They might annoy you or upset you, but she must never see it.

If she asks you tough questions, either answer them honestly or explain that it's none of her business.

If she acts irrationally or in a way you don't like, make your feelings clear without yelling or becoming upset yourself.

She really does want to see and feel that you're your own person and able to react sensibly to the emotional upsets of others. That knowledge will bring her far more comfort than any amount of money, affection, or unsolicited compliments ever could.

SCORE

SCORE INDICATORS OF INTEREST

There is one question I get asked over and over again by both men and women: *"How do I know if he/she likes me?"*

The advice I give women is pretty cut and dry: If he's talking to you, then he's interested.

For men, it's less black and white and more like a gradient of grey. At one end of the spectrum, *she really likes you;* at the other end of the spectrum, *she's completely uninterested.* By the way, you may have noticed I didn't say that hate was the other end of the spectrum simply because a woman can completely hate you and still be very interested in you.

Many women, even when very interested in you, will fear your rejection and therefore be too shy to be obvious about their interest.

Plus, most women will prefer indirect over direct IOIs. Being obvious isn't something they prefer. While most guys think being open and direct ("Hey, I think you're hot") is the best approach, most women feel being indirect is best (she glances in your direction, then quickly looks away).

It's a rare event when a woman will simply come out and tell you she's interested. This is why we men must learn to see and interpret a woman's indirect expressions of interest.

I've found there are really two mindsets that are optimal when first learning to read a woman's interest:

👍 Pay attention to the subtleties of her communication.

Assume she's interested.

If a woman is too shy to directly express her interest, the very best approach is to assume she's interested.

Why? Because if she's interested and you assume she's interested, you're moving things forward naturally.

If she's not interested and you assume she is, when you continue to escalate, it's actually possible she could become more interested simply because she's enjoying the escalating interaction.

The worst-case scenario is that she's forced to be more direct about her disinterest. Some guys might think the added effort spent flirting with a woman who turns out to be uninterested is a waste of energy and might even be something to feel embarrassed about. I'm telling you now that it doesn't have to be interpreted this way.

This bit of invested time could have provided you with huge gains especially if a woman turns out to be the woman for you. Taking the time to flirt with her is the cost of knowing for sure.

As we discussed earlier, many women will test you before they're willing to become vulnerable enough to show you their interest. Sometimes this is called her *bitch shield* because it's meant to repel most of the men who are hitting on her. It's your job to ignore her bitch shield.

While most guys will never know a woman's true self because they don't have the nerve to ignore her negative reactions, you can be that one guy who's willing to see her shield as simply a useful defense system that keeps her safe from annoying or dangerous men.

Just assume it's on until either she's either said "No, thanks" or you've lost interest.

Pay attention to the subtleties of her communication.

The least important thing a woman communicates is what she says.

I can hear all of my female readers gasping in unison. Before you rage at me, let me explain.

Think of what we communicate in terms of the Three Vs: Verbal, Vocal, Visual.

Albert Mehrabian (a Professor Emeritus of Psychology at UCLA) has given seminars worldwide explaining his findings regarding human communication. He explains that words account for 7% of our message, tone of voice accounts for 38%, and body language accounts for 55%.

We will come across as consistent and therefore trustworthy and attractive only when *what* we're saying matches *how* we're saying it.

Have you ever noticed how ironic a car salesman seems when he's giving you a big fake smile? His words don't match his body language.

Men and women communicate by means of the Three Vs. The problem is that women spend their entire lives paying attention to all three aspects of communication while we men tend to focus only on the words being said.

If you learn to start paying attention to the three ways in which a woman communicates with you, you'll be that much faster in discerning whether or not she's interested.

Verbal Indicators of Interest:

- She starts a conversation with you.

- She helps the conversation when there are pauses.

- She gives you compliments ("You're so hot!" "You have an amazing smile!" "I love the way you laugh!").

- She says, "You're so funny!"

- She says, "You're kinda crazy!"

- She teases you in some way, gives you a nickname ("Hair Guy"), or pretends she hates your shoes.

- She asks you a lot of questions. "What's your name? How old are you? Where do you live? What do you do? Are you single?"

- She tries to agree a lot with whatever you're saying. This is her seeking your approval and rapport.

- She says things like, "I can't believe I'm telling you this but ..."

Non-Verbal Indicators of Interest:

- 👍 She makes strong eye contact with you.

- 👍 She fidgets or acts nervous.

- 👍 She fixes her hair and makeup a lot.

- 👍 She smiles at you.

- 👍 She smiles a lot in general.

- 👍 She touches her necklace or breasts unconsciously.

- 👍 Her pupils dilate while looking at you.

- 👍 She laughs at all of your dumb jokes.

- 👍 She playfully acts mad and hits you.

- 👍 She stands closer and closer to you without realizing it.

- 👍 She floats around your vicinity hoping you'll notice her.

- 👍 She touches you for any reason. Touching is huge. The more intimate the touch, the deeper her interest.

- 👍 The way her body is facing you: Over time, if she's very interested, she'll start to mimic your body language (crossing legs, sitting towards you, etc.)

- 👍 She leans into you while talking.

Other Indicators of Interest:

- 👍 She calls you more than you call her.

🖑 She texts or emails you often.

🖑 She continues to give you compliments.

🖑 She wants to challenge you or tease you.

🖑 She always returns phone calls.

🖑 She leaves obvious messages on your Facebook or myspace page (with the hopes that others girls get the hint, like, "Hey, I had a great time last night!")

🖑 She seems jealous when you talk about other girls.

🖑 She wants to introduce you to her friends and family.

🖑 She's always trying to sleep with you.

🖑 She touches you often and leaves body parts touching you (her leg) when sitting next to you.

As you can see, there are many things she might be saying and doing which communicate her interest in you.

The best approach is to assume she's interested based on a reading of her IOI while continuing to escalate the intimacy between you.

SCORE BANTER

So what is it? Banter is playful, tongue-in-cheek conversation that involves role-playing, teasing, and a kind of verbal tennis.

Banter begins in the schoolyard. We teased the girl we liked; we pulled her hair. With banter, we can tease and chase each other around on a verbal playing field. Banter is fun and helps to create emotional connection via a shared enjoyment of humour and conversation.

Banter works on two levels: the text (that is, what is actually said) and sub-text (that is, what is actually communicated). Let me give you an example:

I SAY: *"Wow, look at all of those groceries you've got. Looks like you got all of the food groups... Oh, except you forgot to get some chocolate."*

I COMMUNICATE: *"Hey, I noticed you."*

SHE SAYS: *"Ha ha, ya, I guess so, eh?"*

SHE COMMUNICATES: *"Hey, are you cool or creepy?"*

I SAY: *"Well don't feel bad, not everybody can be as healthy as me."* I point to my frozen pizza, candy bars, and chips.

I COMMUNICATE: *"I'm funny, and I'm confident enough to mock my own diet."*

SHE SAYS: *"Ha ha ha, looks like you didn't forget the chocolate food group!"*

SHE COMMUNICATES: *"You're funny, and I'll play along."*

I SAY: *"Well, you still have time to grab some goods."* As I point to the candy bars.

I COMMUNICATE: *"I'll keep playing along because you're fun."*

SHE SAYS: *"Oh no, I really shouldn't."*

SHE COMMUNICATES: *"I'm smiling because this is fun."*

I SAY: *"Go ahead, I promise I totally won't judge you."* (*wink*)

I COMMUNICATE: *"I like this game. Can you keep up?"*

SHE SAYS: *"I starting judging you the moment I saw your PC brand of frozen pizza. Ha!"*

SHE COMMUNICATES: *"I can tease you back because I like you."*

I made the comparison between banter and tennis because when you first start to banter with a woman, you're playing the game as opponents. And if you have the mindset of "is this girl good enough to play with me?" she'll have to keep up with you before you're really hooked. This is one of the reasons it's so powerfully attractive for a woman to meet a guy who's willing to playfully challenge her.

A very beautiful woman who is constantly approached by creepy men will be used to guys approaching her with the mindset that she's the prize and they need to qualify themselves to be worthy of her. As soon as she picks up this sub-text, she'll automatically become disinterested.

A beautiful woman has learned to play her game from a place

of advantage and, more often than not, has become bored with her role. When you challenge her with banter, you'll surprise and interest her.

Once she's figured out she's attracted to you and feels safe with you, you can eventually transition her attraction into rapport and long-term comfort. Banter works for strengthening a relationship at any stage.

Banter with men and women.

We guys banter with each other all the time. Bantering between men is about playful insults and challenging each other's weaknesses. It communicates, "Hey, I trust you enough as a personal friend that I can insult you and you can insult me and we're both totally okay with it."

It's like a verbal high five that says, *"Hey, I think you're pretty cool."*

Banter between men and women is different: it's about flirting, teasing, and affection.

Banter helps you display:

- 👍 Higher social value

- 👍 High self-esteem

- 👍 Confidence

- 👍 Creativity

- 👍 Intelligence

- 👍 Sense of humour

Banter can be used as a way to break the ice with a woman you want to talk to; as an opener, banter can communicate that you're a fun guy, don't take yourself too seriously, and more importantly, don't take her too seriously. Plus, it's a personal, playful, and non-threatening way to get to know each other.

Banter is a valuable social skill that really takes time to learn. If you want to know how to banter, sit at a bar and watch a bartender banter with patrons and employees. Bartenders are usually well-practiced and effective at bantering.

SCORE FUN: BANTER AND ROLE-PLAYING

Role-playing is the sharp edge of your bantering sword.

Bantering role-play with a woman can be like foreplay if it's done well.

Here's an example of role-playing banter:

Interaction between my waitress and me:

> **ME:** *"Wait a minute... I didn't order this."*
>
> **HER:** *"Oh crap. That's right, you ordered this Diet Pepsi. Here ya go."*
>
> **ME:** *"Wow, you're not a very good waitress are you?"* I grin.
>
> **HER:** *"Watch it or I'll turn on you."* She winks.
>
> **ME:** *"It's like you hate me or something. Wait... did you take a drink from this glass already? There's lipstick..."* I raise my voice dramatically and with a smile.

HER: *"Ha ha ha, ya, I've been busting my ass all day and was desperate for a taste of aspartame."*

ME: *"Does this mean I should be ordering a bigger meal with the expectation you'll be eating my fries?"*

HER: *"Well, duh. Actually, I'm hoping you have a craving for our new Deva Salad because I love it!"*

ME: *"Oh man, I know how awkward this can be in front of our friends and everything... but I think we need to break up. I had no idea how high maintenance you are!"*

HER: *"Well ever since you started snoring in your sleep, I've kind of been sabotaging our relationship anyways."*

ME: *"I knew it when you got all weird last night. It's too bad too because I really love your mom. Perhaps we should reconsider for the sake of the kids?"*

HER: *"Ya, little Timmy really deserves a dad in his life."*

My married friends who witnessed this exchange were thinking "What the f*** is happening here?"

If you're going to role-play with a woman, assume you're the prize and she's trying to get your attention.

For example:

ME: *"Ha ha ha, I can't believe you just stepped on my foot like that! You're such a brat!"*

HER: *"Oh, my god, I'm sorry, I didn't even realize! Wait...ha ha ha, did you just call me a brat?"*

Dating guru David DeAngelo suggests calling a woman brat as a tease. I've since heard it throughout the online dating community. The word brat frames a woman as the annoying little sister and you as the older brother she's constantly trying to get approval from.

Beautiful women never have men looking down at them like annoying little girls, so when a man calls a beautiful woman "brat," he's implying that he sees himself of higher status but with a playful touch of familiarity and humour. Women enjoy this kind of playfulness and fun, and it puts you in a place of authority. This is powerful.

SCORE CONGRUENCE

So what does it mean to be congruent and why does it matter?

CONGRUENT:

n: corresponding in character or kind.

I believe that one of the most powerful ways for any man to be attractive to any woman is to simply be congruent. So let's look closer at this concept of congruence.

Being congruent is about aligning what you say with what you really mean and with what your body language is communicating. In other words, everything about you must say the same thing. When what you communicate comes across as inconsistent, those around you become suspicious about your character and intentions.

Let's say you're a nice guy and you start talking to a woman at the counter next to you; she unconsciously pays attention to your body language, your gestures, your breathing patterns, your vocal tone, and the words you're saying. If you're smiling with your mouth but not with your eyes, she'll suspect you're hiding something. You'll come across as creepy. Car salesmen are famous for this. If the words coming out of your mouth seem rehearsed or memorized, she'll sense you're being a fake.

Imagine you're a fitness trainer at a gym except you're about 100 lbs overweight. People will be far less likely to trust you as a trainer because you're displaying incongruence.

This concept works both ways. Our self-esteem is closely linked to how congruent our actions are with our beliefs about ourselves. If you see yourself as being a strong healthy man yet can't say no to over-eating or can't drag yourself to the gym, you're acting incongruently with your beliefs about yourself; as a result, your self-esteem suffers.

The opposite is also true. If you see yourself as being a man of purpose and you consistently act upon your life goals, you'll have a deep sense of personal power and self-trust because of this inner-congruence.

Learn to get your inner game in line with your outer game. Address your inner issues; find resources, books, people, or friends who can help you.

It's more effective for your long-term happiness to address your insecurities than it is to pretend they don't exist. You can't free yourself from the weeds in your garden by pretending they're not there—you must go into the garden and pull them out!

SCORE BOUNDARIES

Do you know what the largest organ is in the human body?

It's not the heart, lungs, brain, or even the lower intestines.
It's the skin. Skin is the protective boundary that regulates the body's relationship between the inside and the outside. If you consider that skin receives about 1/3 of the blood circulating through our bodies, you can appreciate its importance to our well-being.

As we've evolved socially, we've also developed social boundary systems which help keep us secure in our interactions with others.

One such boundary system is called *personal space*. There seem to be specific distances we unconsciously maintain for different kinds of interactions. In 1966, Edward T. Hall developed the term *proxemics* to describe the measurable distances between people as they interact.

He defined *intimate space* (1.5 feet or less), *personal space* (4 feet or less), *social space* (12 feet or less), and *public space* (25 feet).

If we think about what we do in our intimate space, such as whispering, touching, and kissing, obviously this space is very close to the body.

Personal space is an arm's length away from you. This is reserved for handshakes and one-on-one conversations. This is a comfortable talking distance. This is the distance you and a woman seek to maintain comfortably when talking for the first time.

There are deeper psychological boundaries you should be aware of when trying to build rapport with a woman. Without these boundaries, we allow others to drain us of energy and influence us negatively.

Let's say these psychological boundaries define our emotional body—i.e., our psychological well-being and self-esteem.

A healthy emotional body is very important for attracting women. A man with no boundaries will eventually and increasingly have trouble attracting and keeping an emotionally healthy woman.

Boundaries also define the dividing line between what we can control (what goes on inside and what we allow inside) and what we cannot control (e.g., the behaviour of others).

When I'm feeling sad, that falls within my boundaries because I can control that; if you're feeling sad, that falls outside of my boundaries because you control that.

Problems arise when we think we're responsible for the control of someone else's emotional body. Sometimes, for example, we are so empathetic that we confuse other people's feelings as our own. While it is within our control not to try and hurt someone through our actions and behaviours, we can't control or change how others interpret our actions and behaviours.

Here is a list of things within my control:

👍 My feelings

👍 My thoughts and actions

👍 My rules and reasons

👍 My preferences (the things I like and dislike)

Here is a list of things outside of my control:

👎 The feelings and emotions of others

👎 The thoughts and actions of others

🖒 The rules and reasons of others

🖒 The preferences of others

🖒 All external, uncontrollable factors in the world, like traffic and the weather

When you waste your time and energy trying to control things outside of your control, such as the actions of others, you're only inviting suffering and disappointment into your life.

Have you ever made a date with a woman who seemed totally into you? You called her and made plans and you spent an hour and a half grooming yourself, showering, and getting dressed so that you looked your very best; then you showed up at the restaurant an hour early so that you could get a great table. You waited and you waited, and after two hours, you realized she wasn't going to show up.

Did you get upset?

Did you take it personally?

I bet dollars to donuts you'd be far less traumatized by such an occurrence if you understood that her actions are not a reflection of you personally, nor are they within your control.

This interpretive boundary does a lot for us, actually. You likely have a lot of insecurities if you have weak boundaries and, by extension, a weak emotional body. A man with strong boundaries, on the other hand, does not allow insecurities to dictate how he lives and relates to other people.

Guess which guy gets the girl? The one who lets women walk all over him or the confident guy with well-defined boundaries?

The man with the healthy emotional body, who radiates self-confidence, will be the most attractive to women.

Why?

I think we've established that women prefer a man of direction, personal strength, honesty, and confidence. That perfectly describes a man with healthy personal boundaries. He knows what he can control in his life, and what he can't. He lets women know where he stands on certain behaviours. He has rules about how people treat him, and he enforces these rules.

> *"We teach people how to treat us."*
> *~ Dr. Phil*

The opposite would be a man with weak boundaries. This man is an insecure, over-protective, controlling jerk who thinks he should have control over others or else he's an insecure nice guy who has no boundaries (or doesn't insist on them) and lets women walk all over him. In both cases, he has unhealthy personal boundaries.

How do we create strong healthy boundaries?

You must come to accept the things in your life that are within your control. This includes everything within your mind, your thoughts, and your actions. That's it. It's not much, really.

The fastest way to establish your boundaries with your friends and the women you date is to simply deny everything, at least at first. This is a very powerful exercise if you've never done it before.

When someone asks you to do something, simply say no.

HIM: *"Hey, buddy, can you pick up this tab for me? I don't want to break a twenty."*

YOU: *"No. Don't be cheap and pay for yourself, dude."*

HER: *"Hey sexy, wanna buy me a drink?"*

YOU: *"You buy this round; I'll get the next one."*

HER: *"I want you to take me to see that new movie that just came out this Friday."*

YOU: *"No. But I'm free Thursday."*

HER: *"Tell me how old you are."*

YOU: *"No. But if you guess right I'll buy the next round; otherwise, you buy the next round."*

HER: *"Awesome, pick me up at 7!"*

YOU: *"No. I can pick you up at 7:30."*

Simply practicing saying no will really change how you see yourself and how others see you. Only once you've proven to yourself that you can maintain your own boundaries by saying no to everyone, can you start to rewrite your new boundaries.

Each no is a step towards defining your boundaries. People actually love a man with boundaries. It's spectacularly powerful.

SCORE YOUR OWN PURPOSE

If you pay attention to all the high-quality women you meet, especially when they're in love, you'll discover a pattern of the type of guys they're attracted to. They want to be with a guy who's on his own path, who knows his own purpose.

In reality, no woman wants to be her man's number one priority. She may want to be his number one woman but never his number one priority. When a man is focused and determined and fulfilled by the life he's living, he generates a type of completeness about himself that women are naturally attracted to.

A man dedicated to his own purpose is an attractive man. When a man forges toward his own purpose, he creates a kind of gravitational pull that draws others to him.

The opposite is also true. When a man has no purpose, he becomes an energy vampire. When a man doesn't know where he's going, he tends to become an anchor for those he latches onto. A woman doesn't want a man to latch onto her, dragging her down. She wants a man who has energy and direction.

If you're directionless, your priority should be yourself. Before you can attract women, you must feel attractive to yourself. Find your purpose. Discover what brings you a feeling of accomplishment each day, week, and year. When you're passionate about what you're doing with your life, you'll find it far easier to draw the attention of everyone you meet.

There's something inherently alluring about someone who's distracted by their own life's passions. Just look at how easy it is for musicians and artists to draw people into their lives through their work. We love seeing passion in people.

Become passionate about anything and it will infuse your conversations with the women you meet. Be focused on your passions instead of on every hot woman who crosses your path. Having a life purpose frees you from becoming desperate for a woman's attention, approval, and comfort— desperation will only push women away.

⌫ **Go Online For Resources & Links For This Section:** www.IgnoreAndScore.com/Rapport

⌫ **Questions About This Section? Email Me Here:** questions@IgnoreAndScore.com

CORE BEHAVIOUR: ESCALATION

WHAT IS ESCALATION?

ESCALATE:

v: to increase in intensity, magnitude, etc.

If you fly into a conversation with a woman all hot and bothered, bombarding her with your sexual interest, you'll scare her away. If, on the other hand, you take your time expressing your interest, you'll give her room to both get to know you and familiarize with your presence, interest, and touch.

So what is escalation when it comes to dating and women? Each step you make, from asking her out on a date to holding her hand to kissing her to rounding home base, takes incremental steps, each one slightly more intimate than the last.

You can't make huge jumps without freaking her out, so the easiest path to dating success is to simply take each step slowly, carefully, but confidently.

Let me teach you something fundamental about women: They won't escalate.

Why?

Because that's your job.

Ultimately, women are drawn to men who lead. Women want to be appreciated, looked at with hunger, and ultimately seduced. She doesn't want to feel responsible for the dirty things the two of you might end up doing together. If she can explain away her actions with, "Oh, well, he simply seduced me into bed," she'll have no guilt, regret, or fear of the judgment of her girlfriends and therefore very little resistance to your escalation.

What stops men from escalating with the women they date?

Fear. It's the oldest cock-block in the book.

We fear we'll scare her away by being too aggressive, or we fear embarrassment and rejection. Let's examine some irrational thinking that may prevent us from taking action.

Irrational Thought: If I make a move and she stops me, I'll lose all the ground I've gained to this point! I don't want to have to start all over!

The Truth: If a woman stops you while you're escalating, you haven't lost any of the ground that led up to that point. It simply means she wants to wait until she feels more trust and comfort. The best thing is to take a small step back, give her emotional body space to relax, and then, when she's comfortable, it's your job to slowly start escalating again.

Irrational Thought: If I try to kiss her now, she'll think I'm just a horny jerk!

The Truth: She'll feel far worse if you never try to kiss her. Women want you to desire them, and if you don't even try to escalate, she'll assume either you're not interested or that she's undesirable. She might still stop you from escalating, but she'll likely never blame you for trying in the first place.

Irrational Thought: If I keep escalating, I'm being domineering, and I think that's worse than being patient and letting her decide when it's the right time.

The Truth: There's a huge difference between being dominate (which women prefer) and being domineering (which healthy women hate). If you're escalating because you're ultimately trying to control her or trying to manipulate her with fear and aggression, you need to stop and immediately seek professional help. If, on the other hand, you're simply being a healthy sexual creature who's trying to lead a woman into an emotionally and sexually satisfying interaction, she'll either follow you or she won't. You'll never know until you try.

You must understand that most women have absolutely no desire to lead their relationships. A woman wants to choose the man she dates, but she wants him to lead her on the dating adventure.

This means she will never walk across a room to come chat with you no matter how sexually interested she is. Most women simply don't have the heart to risk rejection, especially in a social scenario. She simply won't do it, no matter how great your eye contact is. The most she'll do is create attractive eye contact, smile, or converse with you if you converse with her first. Sometimes she'll even orbit your location with the hope that her proximity will draw you to her.

This means it's in your hands to lead the seduction. It's your job to cross that room; it's your job to get her number; it's your job to take her hand, hug her, kiss her, and everything else that follows.

It's your job to always be putting your heart on your sleeve with the very real risk of being rejected.

When I say you need to always be escalating, I mean it. It's your job to always be (carefully) moving the relationship forward. If you wait for her to give you the right signal, you'll never make it happen.

IGNORE

IGNORE YOUR URGE TO GO FAST

Let's review the magic formula: Take two steps forward and one step back.

When you take two steps forward in a gradual escalation of physical intimacy between you and your date, her emotional body will sense the incursion. If she's attracted to you, this sensation is what she actually wants; however, despite her attraction, she may still feel tense and worried about what will happen if she opens up to you.

If you rush the process of escalation, you'll communicate to her that you're like a high school boy with no self-control, whose only goal is sexual satisfaction.

This makes you seem weak and possibly dangerous.

Women need to feel seduced.

If you're racing to get into her pants, you're shutting out any possibility of her anticipating your moves toward intimacy; this may fatally affect her desire for you and your chances with her.

Seduction takes time, patience, and the tension of a push/pull dynamic.

IGNORE YOUR DESIRE TO BE DIRECT

Women are like magicians; they're always trying to misdirect you.

Often they'll say one thing but mean another. It's your job to see past what she says to what she's really trying to say.

For example, a woman might be very interested in you but act completely disinterested. She might make a date with you and completely flake out and cancel at the last minute, even if she's completely into you. As a matter of fact, often the more interested she is, the less she'll show it.

On the other hand, we guys tend to be very obvious about what we mean and what we say. Therefore, a woman's subtle and even contradictory way of communicating can be really confusing.

Here are some subtle ways to express to a girl that you like her:

> "Hey, do you have email? Good, write it down and write your number down, too."

> "Hey, I'm going to grab myself a tea at the local bookstore tomorrow night after 6; are you interested in going with me?"

> "Hey, you have great hair."

> "I really like your shirt."

> "I can't believe you just said that! You're such a brat!"

> "I had a great time, thanks! Have a good night." – followed by a goodnight kiss

Here is the wrong way to tell a girl you like her:

> *"Ha ha ha, you're so funny! Seriously, most women just aren't funny! Oh God, please tell me you're single!?"*

> *"I LOVE your hair! Wow, you're really beautiful. Jesus, have you ever modeled?"*

> *"Um, so did you have a good time tonight? I had such an amazing time! Well, I hope I can see you again! What do you think?"*

As much as women complain that men are confusing and hard to understand, the truth is we're not. Most guys are too insecure to be honest about how they feel or else they're too obvious about how they feel.

The sweet spot for women is to be honest and subtle.

One of the most powerful things you can do is leave a woman wanting more of you, with some uncertainty as to what you really think of her.

When I first started dating, I thought it was my job to remove any doubt from a woman's mind as to how I felt. I figured most women were too nervous or shy and simply needed my reassurance that I was interested. This means I ended my dates by assuring them how much I liked them while desperately trying to make plans for our next date.

Over-doing it like this destroys a woman's desire for you; it tells her exactly how you feel about her, which gives her no reason to wonder and think about you.

If, on the other hand, you simply ended the date with a smile and a kiss but without spilling your guts and even without making a next date, it leaves her slightly unsure about how you feel about her. This instills a tiny seed of doubt, which means you'll be on her mind for the next few days even if, at first, she had little interest in you at all. This alone gives you miles of advantage over any other guy she might have met that week.

Ignore your need to reassure her of your intentions; instead, escalate with your actions. Don't bother telling her endlessly how great she is and how much time you want to spend with her. Instead, simply spend more time with her. Let your actions speak for you.

IGNORE YOUR INSECURE REACTIONS

Women suffer from far more social judgment than men ever will. There is really no male equivalent to slut, whore, bitch, skank, tramp, easy, frigid, loose, etc.

We grow up on the schoolyard learning the different ways girls can be judged, with a very heavy emphasis on her sexual promiscuity or lack thereof.

If you want to insult a guy, you simply call him a girl.

Women learn to be very guarded because of this and very aware of the way others judge their sexual behaviour.

This is demonstrated in just about any survey that asks men and women to divulge how many sexual partners they've had. In every study, women always divulge a lower average number of sexual partners than men (despite the fact that the information is gathered anonymously).

The University of Michigan wrote a detailed report (2006) on this very phenomenon. Another great article on this subject is Sex and Selective Memories (New Scientist, 2003).

Basically, my point is this: Women want sex just as much as we do; they simply go about expressing their desires in a different fashion than we do. A man can be loud, drunk, and outwardly sexual to the approval of his male friends; a woman, on the other hand, must be more reserved and cautious. While our guy friends will high-five us if we're sexually adventurous and promiscuous, women suffer the social judgments and frowns of their friends for the exact same behaviour.

In other words, a woman will simply not give you the outward signs of interest you're sometimes looking for. She simply won't say, *"I like you,"* or, *"Let's have sex tonight."* This is why it's so important to learn to read a woman's behaviours and body language instead.

Women will say things like, *"I don't sleep with guys on the first date,"* or *"I don't like guys with hair on their chest,"* or *"I would never let a guy video tape me having sex with him,"* and yet women do these things all the time. This confused me at first.

Why tell a guy you're not going to sleep with him if you really are going to sleep with him? Or why have I heard many women say, *"I would never date a guy who cheated on me"* only to see her do exactly that?

Women consciously don't want to be easy, and they certainly don't want to do anything that might cause other women to judge them as slutty.

This is why most women will simply not come up to you in a bar and tell you they want to have sex with you. The crazy truth of the matter is that most women want to have sex as much as men do, except they feel a very real social straitjacket holding them back from acting upon these feelings, at least outwardly.

You must learn that when women resist you or when they tell you things like, *"I would never do that,"* they're simply stating what's socially expected of them.

If you really want to know if a woman is interested in you, learn to interpret her indicators of interest and be willing to lead her where she wants to go.

If a woman says she doesn't kiss a guy on the first date, accept and appreciate her position. If you really do want to kiss her, you must go through all the same motions you would if she said, *"I always kiss a guy on the first date!"*

Unless she says no or stop, you're safe to assume she simply means not right now.

If she says, *"I never kiss a guy on the first date,"* she really means, *"I don't want to be judged as a slut, and if I don't kiss you on the first date it's because I'm simply not ready to yet."*

Her resistance should be an expected part of your seduction.

If you react by feeling rejected and think things like, *"Poor me, I'm not good enough for her, and she's just a cock tease anyway,"* I guarantee you won't be successful.

If you don't try to kiss a woman within the first three dates, she'll assume you're not interested no matter what else you do or say. If you haven't tried to sleep with her in the first ten dates (it really only takes three), she'll assume you're either not interested or that there's something medically wrong with you.

It's not about what she says, it about what she does. She might say *"I don't want to kiss you,"* but her body might say something very different.

Learn to read her body language. Does she lean into you? Does she mirror your movements? Does she sit across from you, copying your posture? Do her eyes seem extra wide when you're talking? Does she laugh at your lame jokes? These are indicators that she's interested in more.

Her resistance is her way of protecting herself against both physical and social hazards. It's your job to respect her need for safety and to always be escalating.

SCORE

SCORE INTIMACY

INTIMACY:

- *The state of being intimate*

- *A close, familiar, and usually affectionate or loving personal relationship with another person or group*

- *An act or expression serving as a token of familiarity, affection, or the like: To allow the intimacy of using first names*

- *Sexual intercourse*

I think that most men seek relationships with women specifically in search of a unique type of intimacy; some men are only seeking sex; others seek a more emotional connection.

In the end, we all share the same goal: intimacy with women.

Intimacy is really a deeper level of rapport and comfort. Dating intimacy is about taking the comfort you're developing and escalating it.

Since this eBook is specifically about dating, I am writing with the assumption that you'll eventually want to have sex with her.

There's a saying I've heard and have first-hand experience in:

If you want a girl to be your girlfriend, simply have sex with her.

The truth of this quote is that most women become connected and attached to men they've enjoyed having sex with. Please notice that I said, *"They've enjoyed having sex with,"* because if she's had a bad sexual encounter with you, she'll likely not want to have another.

Again, when a woman ultimately opens herself up to a sexual encounter with you, she's letting herself be vulnerable with you. If, during this time, you've proven that you won't hurt her and that you'll treat her with care and awareness, she'll both appreciate you and likely yearn for more of you.

This is why it's so important for you to understand what intimacy is to her and how you can escalate, amplify, and share it.

Through honesty, leadership, escalation, and enough patience to take a step back once in a while, you can easily develop a connection with just about any woman.

SCORE VULNERABILITY

Some people maintain very rigid barriers around their emotional bodies to protect themselves further damage. These barriers may feel safe and secure, but they also prevent a person from experiencing real intimacy with others.

To enjoy an enduring and emotionally-charged sexual encounter, you must take the time to remove your emotional barriers.

You've spent a lifetime building barriers, but they work against you in the bedroom. To truly connect with a woman, you must show her you're willing to let down your guard. You must be able let down your guard before she'll feel comfortable and safe enough to let down hers.

When you're dating, it's important for her to see how strong you are. In other words, you must be willing to take risks and show leadership and courage. Women gravitate towards men who appear strong and self-assured; however, a truly strong man is able to take the risk of opening himself up to intimacy and vulnerability.

Women fantasize about meeting a man who's strong and brave, yet one whom she's able to humble in the private intimacy they share. Read any romance novel, and you'll see the underlying theme: Woman tames the untamable.

Don't misunderstand what I'm saying here. Women want to know you have depth and real emotions, but they don't want you to continuously expose them. Your woman wants to discover you over time and with much effort. She doesn't want you to unload all of your insecurities and emotional troubles onto her shoulders; she doesn't want you to seek her approval, protection, or forgiveness. This isn't the way to attract a woman.

She does want to have access to you in a way that no other person has, but she wants to work for this access over time.

Women have told me time and again that they want to have sex with a man who's proven his strength outside the bedroom yet is willing to open up and be vulnerable with her inside it.

Here's another aspect to intimacy and vulnerability you should always practice: When a woman finally opens up and becomes vulnerable with you, it's your job to suddenly become completely non-judgmental. The opposite of caring is judging. If she feels judged when she's vulnerable, even for a second, she'll likely never open up to you again. You'll see married couples with terrible troubles simply because they never learned to respect each other's vulnerability.

For example, let's say a woman opens up and shares some intimate story with you about her being with another woman. Perhaps she's never told anyone for fear of being judged, yet she's suddenly compelled to share that story with you. From that point on, if you two ever discuss her secret, you must never use it against her, like in a later heated argument. This means keeping her secrets truly secret (sharing or bragging with your buddies is not cool) and never using her secrets against her later in the relationship.

Also, when she's naked, it's bad to do the following:

- Frown or act disappointed with what you see.

- Tease her, unless it's a compliment (e.g.: "This is awkward …you're WAY hotter than me…").

- Criticize her in any way ("Wow, you tan too much").

- Laugh at her moles, freckles, or other superficial marks.

- Suggest ways she could improve her sexual skills. (This is something to chat about outside the bedroom or, if it's not your first time together and you've developed a comfortable rapport, in a manner that doesn't make her defensive or embarrassed, such as, "Would you mind doing this…?").

When she's opened up and becomes vulnerable, either through an intimate discussion or possibly when she's naked during sex, it's your job to encourage her.

Appropriate and sincere compliments actually work the best

when she's vulnerable, such as telling her how beautiful each part of her body is, how perfect her smell is, and how great she tastes. Her greatest fears become amplified when she's vulnerable, so it's your job to make sure she feels safe, loved, and appreciated.

This is the only time I'll say this: The bedroom is the only place to give her your complete approval. Outside the bedroom, it's okay to let her work for your approval, but when she's opened herself up in the privacy of a sexual encounter with you, it's not okay to criticize, judge, or expect more when she's not comfortable enough with you to say *no*.

If there's something she's doing in the bedroom that you want to address in any type of critical way, you must wait until you're removed from the vulnerability of the sexual act.

Use Honesty to Open Up

I truly believe real intimacy can't take place unless you're being totally honest about who you are and how you feel.

If you're feeling guarded, you'll block any real connection. Women use their *bitch shield* and men use their tough guy or *player* personas. A woman will go to the bar to meet a real man, but she'll act bitchy in an attempt to repel the 90% of men who are creepy, inadequate, or only interested in sex. A man must know how to bypass her guardedness to get to the real person underneath.

A man, on the other hand, will often go to the bar and pretend to be ultra tough and might use over-the-top pickup lines, but he will push away most women because they usually reject a man whom they feel is being fake.

The problem is that if a man is only acting like a player, he's able to rationalize away her rejection by thinking, *"She's not rejecting me; she's rejecting my fake personality."* Unfortunately, this barrier prevents many women he might legitimately enjoy interacting with from interacting with him in the first place.

The way to lower someone's guard is to show them you've lowered yours. Monkey see, monkey do.

You must be willing to become vulnerable first, even at the risk of hurt and rejection, before she'll feel safe being vulnerable herself.

Listen carefully to this: As men, we should always be willing to lead a woman in the face of possible risk. This is how a man should operate. If you're not brave enough for this, you're not ready for a sexual relationship.

When I say *"lead a woman in the face of possible risk,"* you should always do the following:

- 👍 If you see a large, unleashed dog in your path when walking with a woman, walk in front of her.

- 👍 When you're both about to walk into a dark room, you enter first.

- 👍 Hold her hand and lead her across a crowded room, street, or club.

- 👍 Jump into a pool first.

- 👍 Walk first when walking past some shady individuals.

- 👍 Share secrets first.

- 👍 Talk about embarrassing stories first.

👍 Talk about insecurities first.

👍 Share intimate details about yourself first.

👍 Undress first.

A woman can't feel deep attraction for a man she doesn't respect, and she certainly won't respect you if you keep asking her to test the dangerous waters first.

When you're finally in the stage where you're building rapport, make sure you're able to be open and honest when it counts; otherwise, she won't stick around for long.

SCORE SEXUAL INTIMACY

Sexual Drives

One thing I hear a lot of women complaining about is that "Men only want to have sex," and men complaining that "Women only want to trap men into staying around." So where did this come from? Is it actually based on any truth?

In evolutionary terms, men's bodies have evolved to allow for fast and easy orgasm so that we can have sex with as many women as possible. This gives us the advantage of improved odds of impregnating a woman and therefore guaranteeing the continuation of our genes.

Women, on the other hand, are driven (genetically-speaking) by different needs. If a woman gets pregnant, her genes are more likely to survive if she has the help and support of her baby's daddy. Therefore, her genes benefit more if she's careful about whom she has sex with.

If a woman is able to attract a man who's likely to stay around if she gets pregnant, she's at a greater advantage for the continuation of her genes. Therefore, female sexual drives focus more on finding a permanent mate than finding multiple mates or just any mate who may not stick around to help her with her offspring.

In sum, yes, men love to have sex, and yes, women want men to stay around after sex. Of course, this is far too simple to explain the deeper emotional needs we have as human beings; as such, we need to also evaluate our global needs when deciding what we want from our sexual relationships.

Definition of Sex

In the end, if orgasm is really our only reason for sex, we don't need to date at all! I can have satisfying orgasms every night alone in my cozy little apartment. Why even date?

We date because deep down, we're driven by much more than intercourse. We're driven by the exact same things women are driven by. Despite our genetic differences, we want to connect, we want to be loved, we want to be needed, and we want to share ourselves on a deeper level.

Unfortunately, this deeper connecting is rare.

Sex is much more than the actual physical act. A couple's counselor said something to me a long time ago that really made me rethink my definition of sex.

He said this: *"We make love to our wives 10% in the bedroom and 90% on our feet."*

He explained to me that making love wasn't just the act of sex in the bedroom but all of those little things that take place throughout the relationship that implies a level of intimacy not shared with anyone else: holding hands while in a movie theatre, the quick smiles and loving eye contact while across the dinner table, the hugs when saying hello and goodbye, the love notes emailed to each other, the well thought-out Christmas gifts, and all the other acts of tenderness and thoughtfulness that can only be exchanged between two people when barriers are down.

I propose that sex is not just what happens in the bedroom; it can be any type of intimacy you wish to define it as.

Why is this important? Well, for one thing, if we expand our understanding of what sex really is, we move sex out of the bedroom and into our everyday lives.

Remember how amazing that first kiss was with that woman you were totally into? Include that in your definition of sex.

Holding hands? Include it.

Cuddle on the couch? That's sex.

Making out in the car before your friend's wedding? Sex.

Hot bath together. Sex.

Email love letter? Sex.

All of these "little" things enrich your relationships and make the physical act of sex that much more satisfying and complete.

SCORE TRUST THROUGH ESCALATION

Sex is one of the most emotionally vulnerable times a woman can experience, which can elicit a lot of tension and nervousness for her. Unless you're aware of this, you may injure her emotional body and never even know it.

To safely escalate from seduction to sex, you must build her trust. Here are some Do's and Don'ts when it comes to building a woman's trust:

👍 DO:

LEAD: *Lead her step by step to the act of sex. Show her she doesn't have to worry about knowing what to do because you know what to do. Take her by the hand and direct her without hesitation. The more you lead, the more comfortable she will be. Be assertive and honest but be careful not to pressure her. If you like certain things, say so; if she's not comfortable (read her body language), be prepared to take a step back. However, she'll appreciate your ability to lead, and she'll naturally relax when around you.*

VALIDATE HER: *Give your woman all of your approval and validation when in the bedroom. The best time to give her your entire approval is when she's vulnerable.*

PRAISE HER: *This is about appreciation of her beauty. This is the only place in your relationship that it's okay to put her on a pedestal. Praise her and encourage her to express herself fully and without fear. She's beautiful and you know it, and this is the best place to let her know. If you make her feel good, she'll reward you with emotional and physical pleasures that are far more lasting than the mere physical pleasure of a quick, one-time orgasm.*

LEARN HER BODY: *Read books, go online, or take a course; do whatever it takes to learn what physically pleasures a woman. Ask her what she likes, but more importantly, learn to read her body language. Does she like it when you* *bite the back of her neck? Find out and listen to her body's response. It's your job to learn every single thing that turns her on and what gets her off. Why should she do all the crazy things you want if you don't know how to give her all the physical pleasures she wants? Always pay attention to her body and learn to pleasure it.*

☜ DON'T:

DON'T EVER JUDGE HER: *The very moment you judge a woman for something she likes or dislikes in the bedroom is the same moment she'll close up to you forever. If you use anything a woman says or does in the privacy of the bedroom against her, she'll never trust you again. Trust builds with time but can be lost in an instant. When you're having sex with a woman, she's as vulnerable as she's ever going to be, so there's no room for you to be anything but loving, appreciative, and full of praise.*

DON'T RUSH: *Take your time. Don't be some over-hungry, fat guy rushing to his late night pizza. It's disgusting to see a fat guy slurp up a meal with no appreciation for the taste of it. Take your time and truly appreciate all of the pleasures to be found in exploring each other. If you're a two-pump chump, she'll move on and then joke about you to her girlfriends.*

LET DOWN YOUR GUARD IN THE BEDROOM

As men, we're way behind the curve on this one.

Growing up, I learned that men should never open up or show vulnerability because it makes them look weak. But with time and wisdom, I've learned that the strongest of men are able to open up and show their vulnerability when the circumstances call for it because these same men have a deeper inner confidence.

Why are men and women so guarded when it comes to intimacy? What exactly are they guarding?

We're guarding our insecurities, and when we open up to someone emotionally, we become vulnerable to their judgments and rejection. These are all very serious things. Nobody wants to be rejected when they're exposing themselves openly and honestly.

The more open and honest you are, the more open and honest she'll be. Your bravery, honesty, and open-mindedness will compel her to feel safe and open when she's around you. It's your job to keep your fears in check because when you bring your own insecurities and tensions to the bedroom, you'll only amplify hers.

Go Online For Resources & Links For This Section:
www.IgnoreAndScore.com/Escalation

Questions About This Section? Email Me Here:
questions@IgnoreAndScore.com

CONCLUSION

FINAL THOUGHTS

To attract women, you must **lead**; to build **rapport** and **intimacy,** you must **escalate**. This is the basic framework of my method *Ignore and Score*. We've learned that seduction is a tug-of-war in which resistance is necessary to the game of attraction, both yours and hers.

We've also learned that the push-pull dynamic is the most effective way of attracting a woman; women want neither a man who gives too little of himself or a man who gives too much.

We've learned that women are attracted to a man who knows his own mind, his own destiny. We know that to succeed with women, we must take risks, take the lead, take one step back for every two steps forward, and take it slow. In our intimate lives, we must always be honest and sincere, encouraging and all-approving, strong and vulnerable.

We've rediscovered our confidence—that it's not something we need to acquire but something that's already there inside for us to claim.

We know to ignore our fears and what we can't control; we know to score self-approval, passions, and boundaries. We also understand a woman a little more: why she may resist us and how she demonstrates her interest in us.

And of course, we know to always, **always be escalating.**

The heart of this message is strikingly optimistic: Attracting the woman you want isn't a belaboured process of pretending you're someone you're not, nor is it an undignified process of submitting yourself to a woman's every whim and fancy to gain her approval. In fact, a woman wants the same man you want to be: honest, consistent, deep, empathetic, self-controlled, and confident; this man is at your fingertips because he is who you are.

☞ **Go Online To Find More Links, Videos & Resources: www.IgnoreAndScore.com**

☞ **Questions About This Book? Email Me Here: questions@IgnoreAndScore.com**

MAILBAG QUESTIONS & ANSWERS

ABOUT THIS SECTION

I've received thousands of emails from men and women who read my blog (www.fullofhateandreadytodate.com), and I regularly answer questions at GuysAskGirls.com. This section will include some of my favorite mailbag questions.

GYM FLIRTING AND PICKUP?

QUESTION

First of all, I'm a gym trainer.

I met a girl in the gym. She has a really good personality. She comes to gym every morning, but we've never said hi to each other. I always look over at her, and I've caught her staring at me a couple of times, but when I tried to impress her by lifting weights and then look at her, she turns away quickly (she's probably shy).

I really wanna approach this girl, but I don't know how to. I thought about being her personal trainer (but that would be awkward)? I need some excuses to talk to this girl. How do I start a conversation with her? Any chances of being alone with her?

ANSWER

This is easy. You need to slowly escalate through casual "hellos," then tiny conversations, to finally isolating her outside the gym.

BUT FIRST ask yourself this... should you shit where you eat?

Can you handle dating her, having a horrible breakup, then seeing her flirting with other guys at the gym every day?

If you're a pretty cool and composed dude and you don't think this'll be a problem, then let's move forward. So... escalate.

1) Start With Hello.

Try starting with something like "Hey, good morning." Have a happy/friendly smile on your muscular face. You're a social fun/dude, remember.

Do this a few mornings in a row.

It's so tame that you could do this with the old guy you see each day, too... for practice. Not every move is meant to seduce her into bed... just baby steps, right?

These little "hellos" can eventually blossom into brief morning conversations. She'll assume you're just a friendly guy, but if she thinks you're cute, she'll likely use open and flirty body language... by playing with her hair, by laughing too much at your lame jokes, etc. Or she might be annoyed because she's trying to work out... just pay attention to her reactions and give her space if she looks like she wants it.

I should note: Normally, I'd recommend escalating faster than this, but since you've already seen her at the gym a bunch without saying hello, it's best to start slow. Next time you see a hot girl, immediately start with hello.

2) Get A Spot

Ever ask a dude for a quick spot? Why not her, right? Now, don't ask for a spot with something really heavy .... You don't want to look like you're trying to impress her with your strength. Women don't give a shit how much you can bench. Seriously. Only other dudes do.

This requires that you work out when she's working out. At some point, simply ask her if she can spot you. Perhaps while doing shoulder dumbbell presses.

She might say, "Um… I'm not sure how" or "I don't think I have the strength" to which you can assure her you need very little assistance. Just explain that all you might need is a light touch on your elbows on your final few reps.

I don't know why, but I like this approach.

3) Don't Get Needy

Stay flirty, fun, and open. Don't pressure her to talk when she's busy and don't try to drag out conversations. Just make them fun but short. Remember, she's there to workout, not pickup.

4) Practice

Talk to other people, too, if you're a little shy. This will help strengthen your social confidence, and it'll grow your social proof in the gym (meaning she'll see you talking to other men and women).

5) Chat

Now it's time to start having longer conversations… not just "hello" but something like, "Hey, you seem like you really have yourself together… and I need a woman's opinion on something… wait, are you single?"

She'll say yes or no.

Then say, "Well, I have this buddy who's undecided if he should date this girl from his office, and I've warned him that it can be really messy dating at work… but what do you think?"

See? It's interesting and you get to see if she's single. Plus it's kinda personal. Rehearse this with other women outside of the gym to get a feel for your pacing and delivery.

You're not doing this to pickup women, you're doing it to practice opening strangers in conversation. Asking for someone's opinion on something is gold when it comes to starting fun conversations. Like the waitress who serves you dinner or the greasy fat guy stocking the fruit at the grocer.

When you're all practiced up, try making small talk with this girl at the gym, when it's more appropriate. Maybe when she's done working out and you're both buying a protein shake at the food counter. Maybe when you're both stretching on the mats after working out.

This shows her you're comfortable talking with her, which will make her comfortable talking with you.

If she's stand-offish to guys hitting on her at the gym, this small-talk approach will help her relax... because you're not hitting on her, you're just making interesting conversation. This also lets you start to get a feel for her personality. As you already know (*wink*), she's more than just a great ass with tits... and you're not interested in settling for a bag of hammers. Right?

6) Isolate

If all seems good to this point, invite her to join you for lunch.

Maybe something like, "Hey Susan! Listen, I always like talking to you... join me for lunch this week. There's a cute sandwich and soup place I've been dying to try and I'd hate to go alone." Say it with a smile.

Hope this gets your wheels turning!

FIRST DATE ADVICE?

QUESTION

Hey, Robby, I purchased your book Ignore & Score earlier this spring and read through it once, and I thought your advice was solid! (NOTE: HE'S REFERRING TO THE FIRST PRINTING OF THIS BOOK. THE VERSION YOU'RE READING HAS BEEN UPDATED TO INCLUDE MORE WEB LINKS AND THIS SECTION OF QUESTIONS AND ANSWERS.)

I feel like since I read your book, I've gotten a lot better at being relaxed around the girls I'm interested in. I'm better at not talking about myself as much, keeping her from learning too much about me, and at keeping the conversation fun while not trailing off into something nerdy/geeky.

Anyway, I'm writing to you because I want some of your thoughts on this situation. I've been using a major online dating site for a while with little success. However, I've been revamping my profile every so often and crafting my messages to try and grab a woman's attention.

I came across a woman I'm very much interested in, and I was able to get some messaging going back and forth between us for the last five days until I asked her out to dinner this upcoming Friday evening. She accepted and messaged me her phone number. I messaged her mine back.

Now what do I do? Do I keep messaging her?

Do I not message her and just meet with her for dinner on Friday? What are your thoughts?

Also, I'm re-reading your book and making sure I'm all set for this upcoming date (such as looking my best; well groomed; good hygiene; keeping the conversation fun; appealing to her emotions;

having relaxed, open body language; building tension, etc.). I think I have some initial rapport built by sharing jokes and interests that she's enjoyed so far. I want to make sure I don't fall into the trap of being a nice guy but with no spine.

I also don't want to blow a chance to escalate attraction by physical contact.

One thing I'm not used to is building attraction via physical contact (such as holding a girl's hand at an opportune time, giving her a hug, kissing, etc.). For a first date, what do you think I should look to do when it comes to physical contact, and what cues should I look for?

And the last question I have is, if the date goes well, how soon should I contact her to set up another date? There are so many "rules" regarding how long you should wait to text her, or whether she should text you first, etc. etc. I wonder if you have any thoughts.

Sorry for the essay/multiple questions. I always enjoy reading your insights, Robby, take care.

ANSWER

That's awesome; thanks for reading my book!

I should note something in what you just said... "keeping the conversation fun and not trailing off into something nerdy/geeky." I completely agree with keeping things light and fun, but try to realize something.... when you judge anything about yourself as nerdy or geeky, it sounds like a negative thing. I realize that many of us refer to ourselves as geeky in a proud way, which is fine, but PLEASE don't let yourself become judgmental or negative about your obsessions, passions, or hobbies... even if they might be described as nerdy or geeky.

For example, let's say you're into model trains.
I think it's PERFECTLY cool to talk about them on a first date as long as you keep it calibrated.

Why?

1) Because when you talk about your hobbies, you're going to be excited and passionate and likely more knowledgeable than her. This means your mood will improve, your energy will be positive, and you'll express a level of authority on the subject. In my case, years ago, I was deep into making my own watches and leather cuffs. And it always came up because I would always be wearing one. I would buy watch faces that I liked and I would make heavy leather cuffs for them.

2) It's interesting to hear about something we don't normally hear about... so for a brief period, she might actually enjoy hearing about the underground world of model trains. Or, in my case, leather crafts.

Now realize I said be "calibrated."

That means you can share some insights into your hobbies and passions as long as she's interested... if she's asking questions and paying attention.

As soon as she stops paying attention, is looking around bored, or stops asking questions about it, then drop it and move onto something else.

3) If, in your heart and guts, you're kinda nerdy or geeky, you should embrace it, love it, and share it. Why? Because ultimately you're going to connect better with a girl who likes your nerdy side, not a girl who can't relate.

It's attractive when a guy is comfortable in his own skin, sharing his desires and interests even when he knows it might push her away. It's a great way of filtering out women who aren't good enough for you.

Yes. Whatever banter you had going online, you can continue via text messaging. I happen to be friends with a dude who wrote a book entirely on texting: *Text Appeal.*

But keep it light... because you haven't met her yet and you don't want to become super needy via her cell phone before she has the pleasure of meeting your fine self.

If you're going to text her again, do it between now and your date, and make a reference to something you were already talking about online. For example, I met and struck up a conversation with a girl online because she had some super long rainbow socks that I thought were funny-looking. So before our first date, I texted her a photo from a store I was in and said, "Should I wear these tomorrow night?" The photo looked something like this:

✍ http://www.ignoreandscore.com/socks/

Don't send her anything mushy like, "I can't wait for Friday night!" or "I'm really excited to meet you!" or "I'm so nervous."

This will just tell her you're over committed to her without having even met her yet. Your value goes out the door.

It's okay to be excited or nervous, but you don't need to release that tension by mentioning it.

So keep your text messages short unless she makes them long. I mean, you don't even know what her texting skills are yet. She might not text at all!

All that said, if it's a long wait until your date (more than 3 days), you should touch base with her at least once via text or email just to stay connected and friendly before the date.

Don't let three or four days go by without having talked with her. Your job is to keep the energy going.

Being NICE is perfectly okay. Being too mushy or overly emotional or overly interested is bad. Remember, you're meeting her to find out if she's good enough FOR YOU, not the other way around. You're testing HER, not the other way around.

Compliments are okay when used sparingly and when you're not seeking her approval.

Here's a blog post I wrote once to help remind you:

  www.ignoreandscore.com/niceguys

Since this is the first time meeting you, it's a GREAT opportunity to be overly touchy, in a calibrated way. She doesn't know you, so she'll assume you're just a touchy person.

Remember that touch is a form of intimacy and it builds trust and rapport. Use touch as long as her body language shows approval. If she pulls away or acts funny, take a step back and give her more space. Reacting to her reaction shows her that you're paying attention and that she can relax and trust you more.

As a rule, I always hug a girl hello like she's a long lost friend. I'll even lift her off the ground with my hug... like a friendly bear hug. I can't say I've ever had a girl not hug me when I've had a happy and excited face with my arms out wide. It's natural to hug someone when they do that. And this is a great way to quickly break that first-touch barrier.

Here's an excellent resource for escalating touch:

🖝 www.ignoreandscore.com/escalation/

1) If the date goes great, keep it going. I'll usually line up my date like this…

a) 30-minute coffee at a cute local cake and tea shop.

b) If she's awesome and fun, we'll either sit there all night talking and eating, or I'll transition the date to a new location. Each change of venue creates a subconscious feeling that she's on a new date. If you bounce to three places, it's like you've been on three dates! So I'll move from the coffee house to a nice walk down the street to the many shops for shopping or for real food.

c) I rarely make dates for a Friday, usually because I like to leave my Friday nights open to close friends and events. My dates normally take place on a Sunday or after dinner on a week night, like Wednesday. This way, if she's awesome, I can say, "Hey, are you free at all this Sunday afternoon? I was going to pull out my portable barBQ and have myself a little hot dog picnic at the local park; the weather's supposed to be awesome! Join me!"

d) If the date goes well, you can either already have a next date idea ready to go that you can invite her to near the end of the date… like I just explained above … OR you can just end the date with her wondering if you're going to call.

e) If my date goes well, I'll sometimes end it with, "You know what, I had a great time! I really enjoyed meeting you." Big hug and goodbye. If she says "We should do this again" then I'd say "You're right… hmm… are you free on Sunday afternoon?" If she doesn't say anything, then I'd leave it at that and I'd call or text her the next day.

I've found the most success using the energy of a good conversation to make plans to see her again. She's already happy and in a good mood, so it's a great time to seal the next date. But only do this near the end of the date and calibrate your plans based on her reactions.

If you say something like, "We should do this again. Are you free Sunday?" And she says, "I'm not sure. I'll have to get back to you." That means she's not that interested. So stop trying to make plans and wait for her to show more interest. Basically, a girl who wants to see you again will jump at the chance, not give you "maybe."

Finally

You don't know her yet; don't let your excitement overwhelm your reason. Imagine this situation: You have seven dates with seven girls this week. You need to treat each date knowing you have six more dates to get through. Pace yourself. Don't get over committed just because she's hot or fun or seemingly perfect. Give yourself time to get to know the real her.

Allow her time to impress you. Allow her space to show you her real self.

Dating is about finding a girl who meets YOUR expectations. It's not your job to meet HER expectations. Let her worry about finding her perfect man, even if it's not you.

Your only job is to have fun; if you're making dating stressful, it's not fun anymore.

TRUST ME... it's more attractive to be with a guy who's being sincere and honest and having fun over a guy who's stuck in his head trying to do the right things.

It's OKAY to fuck up.

It's OKAY to scare a girl away if you're a little boring.

It's OKAY to scare a girl away if you tried to kiss her too soon.

Every fuck up becomes a learning lesson, a stepping stone, and a funny story to share with your guy friends.

Dating is about having fun, being excited to meet someone new, and gaining the social skills it takes to become REALLY good with people. When you're good with people, you'll be good with women; that's just how it works

So go out and make as many more dates with as many more women as you find interesting or fun!

Good luck, have fun, and enjoy yourself!

IS BEING DESPERATE THE SAME AS WANTING A RELATIONSHIP?

QUESTION

I think it's happened to most of us who've experienced dating, so what's the main difference between being "desperate" for a relationship or simply wanting a relationship? What are the signs? It seems as if everybody jumps as fast as they can to the conclusion that nowadays everybody is desperate when they might just be trying to get to know someone. You get shut down before having even thought of trying.

ANSWER

It's really the difference between desperation and desire... scarcity vs. abundance... taking vs. giving.

Needy Guy

Guys who are "desperate" for a girlfriend tend to have a scarcity mentality: they think or feel they're lacking something (approval, love, attention, affection, etc.) and they mistakenly think that a girlfriend/relationship will provide what they're lacking.

They make the GIRL the goal.

This is a tragic mistake because this freaks women out. Women don't want to be your crutch or your destination.

These guys think they need to get a girl, and girls avoid them like they're needy beggars asking for change.

Signs you're desperate:

- You call or text her way more often than she does.

- You get upset if she doesn't respond to you instantly.

- You worry that she's meeting other men.

- You try to control her in any way.

- You are always trying to get girls to like you, either with gifts or compliments or simply by being super nice.

- You sit around obsessing about girls.

- You'll keep dating a girl even if she treats you poorly.

- You spend time wishing more people liked you (parents, friends, girls, etc.).

Secure Happy Guy

Then there are guys who have an abundance mentality. They already have such an abundance of love, self esteem, friends, inner affection, and self approval, they don't need it from someone/somewhere else.

Instead of seeking love and approval, they GIVE it.

When a guy with abundance desires a girlfriend, it's not to GET something from her, it's to GIVE to her. He doesn't make a girlfriend his destination; instead, he wants to share his journey WITH his girlfriend to whatever destination he already had. That's one reason women love men who have life passions.

Women don't want to be used as a crutch; they don't want to be used as a bridge to help you feel more secure or happy. Nobody does.

Signs you're secure and happy:

- 👍 You spend most of your time enjoying life and thinking about your career, friends, or passions.

- 👍 Everyone seems to call and text you more than you text them, and you don't seem to notice.

- 👍 People seem to love being around you, but you don't tend to notice.

- 👍 Others seem desperate for your approval.

- 👍 You enjoy meeting beautiful women even when they're not interested in a romantic relationship with you.

- 👍 You like helping others.

Most guys with a scarcity mentality don't take the time to heal their inner/past traumas; they mistakenly think the approval of someone else will heal them instead of taking responsibility for themselves.

So if you're needy or desperate, I suggest doing some inner

game work, spending some quality time alone with yourself, and developing a new positive relationship with YOURSELF that's happy, secure, honest, and sincere. It's the guys who really love themselves that know how to give that same love to women. And women can FEEL this positive energy.

I hope this helps!

NUMBER FIRST OR DATE FIRST?

QUESTION

Okay, so I'm wondering, if you'd like to know someone better, or have feelings for her and want to go on a date, what method would you go for first?

a) Ask her on a date, hoping for her to show up. If she does and you think you suit her, ask for a 2nd date?

b) Ask for her number, call her the next day, and then ask for a date?

c) Or just ask her for a date and if she says yes, then ask her for her number?

ANSWER

1) If you've met a girl and the conversation is going well and she's showing signs of interest (laughing, talking, touching, etc.) then go straight to a meet up. Getting her number will only add another speed bump between now and the date. If you call her later, you're risking her mood being different from when you first met (she might be upset about something else and decide you're creepy instead of awesome). Instead, use the energy during your first conversation to transition right into a date setup.

2) Don't "ask her for a date." It'll almost always come out as

weak or lame.

3) Instead invite her to join you for food or drinks and further conversation.

This: "You know what, you're not what I expected at all! Hey, I'm just heading to Starbucks to grab a pick me up... join me, right now!"
NOT this: "You're pretty cool. Will you go on a date with me?"

Can you FEEL the difference? I promise that she will.

HOW SIMPLE IS IT TO GET A GIRLFRIEND?

QUESTION

How simple is it to get a girlfriend?

I wouldn't know because I've only had one and it was in 5th grade so that doesn't even count.

I'm 20 years old, and everybody gets along with me very well. I'm really funny, and I'm a pretty confident guy. I'm fat, but plenty of fat dudes have gotten laid before me, so what do I have to do?

ANSWER

I'm glad you didn't waste your breath cursing women or blaming society for your current situation. One of the hardest things for me to learn was this: We are each responsible for what happens to us in our lives and what we earn for ourselves.

It's not that you CAN'T get a girlfriend, it's either that you're not really trying (not escalating relationships) OR you don't have the appropriate skills.

And yes, dating and relationships require certain social skills. Nobody is born knowing how to make women attracted to them or how to escalate, etc.

So which is it? Are you unaware of the social skills required, or are you too afraid to apply them?

If you have plenty of friends, you've already proven you have social skills. You are worth knowing. That's the easy part.

Let's be honest... you're not escalating.

Try this ...

1) Meet more women

Be more social.
Force yourself to make friendly conversation with all women... pretty and ugly.

This isn't to get laid. It's to help your body relax and get comfortable in social situations. This is KEY.

2) Lead

When you've met someone you like, after she's shown a little interest back, invite her to join you for food and drinks—either in that very moment or within a few days.

Something like this, "You know what? You're not what I expected when I first started chatting with you. Hey, I'm going to grab a Starbucks just down this street right now... join me for 30 minutes... I want to chat with you some more." If she's busy, say this, "Well, I'll tell you what. There's this super cute cupcake place that serves coffee and biscuits I've been wanting to visit again. Meet me there tomorrow after work!"

Notice I'm not saying, "Will you go on a date with me?" because that's not as effective as, "Hey, join me!"

3) Escalate

Move one tiny step at a time, and you'll find most women have very little resistance.

It's only when you try to escalate really fast that you'll find women get weirded out.

✐ **www.ignoreandscore.com/escalation/**

The easiest way to kiss a girl is to kiss a girl.

 Remember: It's not about making girls like you.

Assume you're an awesome dude that women will naturally like ('cause you're a friendly guy right?). This way, your body will communicate that you're selective and "higher status" because the moment you try to make her like you is the same moment you start acting needy and unattractive.

WAS I BEING WUSSY?

QUESTION

Is it wussy for a guy to send his girlfriend good morning texts, text every day, and ask how her day has gone?

I'm not pushing for sex because she hasn't dated many guys, and I'm a virgin that only wants to sleep with one girl ideally (27 years old, long story). If she seems emotionally distant or unhappy, I try to figure out why and talk about it. We've been dating a month and a half but usually meet 2-3 times a week only.

A female friend read on my phone that I told the girl to 'sleep tight' and said I sounded unmanly and desperate.

Do you think she's right?

I'm 195 cm tall and work out at least twice a week, and I'm not used to any woman calling me unmanly.

ANSWER

I can totally understand your concern. It's super easy to smother a girl with attention when you're really into her.

So don't.
Find the line between seeking her approval and simply being a comforting boyfriend. And trust me... she can sense which energy you're expressing based upon your text or phone call.

Here's a text that sounds wussy: "Hey honey, is everything okay?

Are you doing okay? Let me know if there's anything I can do."

Here's a text that sounds comforting: "Hey Shorty, I hope you're still super cute!"

Always ask yourself this... "Am I sending her this text because I'm desperate for her to like me back or am I sending her this text because I love chatting with her?"

It's really easy to be motivated by our insecurities, which often has the reverse effect of pushing away our partners.

1) The text you described above doesn't actually sound wussy, it sounds fine. Ignore any female friends who are trying to bust your balls about it.

2) If you're unsure how she feels about you, be honest with yourself about it. It's OKAY to not know if she likes you as much as you like her. Accept that you don't know. Accept that you're an awesome dude, likely an awesome loving boyfriend, and that you DON'T need her to like you back.

Realize that if she's WITH you, then she's WITH you.

Don't become needy and desperate because you NEED her to show you how much she likes you.

3) When she's being distant, give her the gift of missing you.

If you're always initiating text messages and she's always just replying, you're playing the role of the chasing boyfriend. And this can be a negative thing when she's showing you she wants distance or when her texts back to you are cold.

So pay attention. By texting and staying in constant contact, you might be killing her reasons to think about you.

Constantly texting a girl can smother her. If her responses are short, that's her trying to tell you to give her space!

If so, text her half as much as you currently do and try to only text in response to something she's done. Let half your texts be in response instead of all of your texts being initiators.

This will help turn the tides from you chasing her to her chasing you. And trust me, she'd rather be chasing you than the other way around!

4) You don't have to have sex to build intimacy and connection. I'm glad you're giving her the sexual boundaries she might need, but that doesn't mean you should stop slowly escalating the sexual vibe of the relationship.

It's okay to flirt and touch and connect without sex. Besides, there's all types of sexual energy you CAN exchange without using your genitals.

5) I've found that keeping the dates down to 2 or 3 times a week helps keep a girl's interest fresh. More than that (before you're both deep into a relationship) can sour her attraction levels just because she's seeing you so much. So pay attention to her interest levels. If her interest in you seems to go cold, see her less often. It's a mistake to try to see her more than she wants.

When she leans away from you emotionally, you NEED to do the same thing!

Giving her space creates a vacuum between you two which will automatically draw her back to you.

6) If all else fails and she moves on, at least you can be proud of yourself for being an honest and sincere dude, which the next girl will surely appreciate.

7) Attraction is about tension. This can come from flirting and teasing and mystery. So if you text her less, see her less, BUT continue to be flirty and escalate, you'll be giving her mixed signals, and this is where the magic of tension comes from.

It'll invite her to wonder how you feel about her, which will put you into her thoughts again and invite her attraction towards you to balloon up. And that's a good thing!

I MISS HER, WHAT CAN I DO?

QUESTION

I miss my ex-girlfriend. It's been two years. What should I do?

I've dated three other girls after her. I'm partying more and doing more things with my life, but I stopped dating those girls because the more I date, the more I miss my ex-girlfriend.

I've told my ex that I just can't get into a relationship with someone else when I still have feelings for her. She told me I should just go out and be someone people can have fun with.

I didn't really respond to that because for me, it's not always about the fun I have with a person, it's about who the person is and what I desire. And it seems like we are so distant compared to how we were (we've been broken up for 2 years now).

Just so you know, she says she's very happy with her current relationship and that she's frustrated that I'm not happy for her. And I do want her to be happy, but at the same time, my heart wants her ... what should I do? I've been distant with her to protect myself and to find myself, but I want to be closer with her.

ANSWER

1) YOUR FEELINGS DON'T MATTER

It sounds like you think your feelings matter, at least in regards to dating and such—specifically your feelings for your ex. It sounds like you're waiting around with the expectation that you'll stop caring about her so that you can "move on" to the next girl.

This isn't always the case, so it's time to acknowledge this.

It's like getting married. You won't suddenly turn gay and find all other women gross.

Your attraction for your ex is perfectly normal, and you should **EXPECT IT!**

If you loved her at one time then OF COURSE you still will. Your feelings for her aren't logical. So it's illogical to be waiting for that to change, because they might not.

Instead you might want accept that you'll always find her attractive. Just like, as a fat guy, I will always find pizza attractive.

The real problem isn't that you still like her, it's that you're wasting time fighting these feelings AND you're wasting time thinking about it, like it's some sort of puzzle.

It's not a puzzle.

There's a reason you're not with her anymore. Who cares what the reason is. It doesn't matter. You're not with her.

Hugs?

2) HEAL AND LET GO

Your emotional body obviously had some injury when you two broke up in the past. The problem you're having now is that you haven't allowed your emotional body to heal, so whenever you're with someone new, you keep her at a distance, like you're protecting the burned skin on your arm. Meanwhile, these new girls are left feeling confused and rejected.

I suggest you take some time for yourself. Get yourself healed. Learn about YOU for a while. Learn what YOU want and need from life. Find your REAL life purpose and passions and start following them.

By the way... a man pursuing his life's purpose is completely alluring to women. He's not distracted by her beauty, and there's something very attractive about that.

In addition, pursuing your purpose will help you heal faster! It keeps your mind busy and your heart happy—two magical ways to heal past hurts.

Find Your Purpose and Women Will Just Show Up

Use your head, not your feelings.

Your feelings will lie to you in order to get what they want: drama. Accept then ignore your feelings so that you can focus on what you KNOW. You deserve to be with someone who wants to be with you. You don't deserve to be chasing some old girlfriend like a creepy stalker.

Whenever you catch yourself sitting around like a pouty baby thinking about your ex, stop it. And immediately do something dramatically different—go golfing or jogging, get busy with close friends. Keep your mind so busy that you don't have time to mull over past dramas. This way, your brain has something healthier to focus on.

Stop dreaming up scenarios where you somehow end up with

your ex. This behaviour is silly and immature and will only continue to hurt you. It feels good because you get to feel sorry for
yourself, but ultimately you deserve better than that!

FIRST DATE LOCATION?

QUESTION

What's your favorite place to take a first date so that she doesn't think you're cheap?

ANSWER

First of all, I never worry about her thinking I'm cheap. I don't even know her yet, so I have no concern for her judgments of me. The moment I get the feeling she's judging me or my choices is the same moment I decide not to see her again.

That being said, I've always preferred something light and interesting.

There are some really decent dessert shops in my city (Edmonton) that serve different cakes and treats along with coffees and teas. This way, our date isn't expensive (it adds up when you go on MANY, MANY dates), and it's not weird if I end the date in 20 minutes (if she's a total loony).

The benefits of a coffee date:

👍 It's affordable.

👍 Who doesn't like eating cake and pie in the middle of day?

- 👍 It's a safe and public place where she doesn't feel isolated or in danger.

- 👍 There's no booze, so she doesn't have to worry about that (I've heard many horror stories from women about this).

- 👍 The shop can be located on a main shopping strip, so if the date goes well, I can invite her to join me for a walk to other stores and adventures.

- 👍 If the date goes badly, it's only a coffee, and I can escape after 20 minutes.

GET A SECOND CHANCE?

QUESTION

How do I get a second chance with this great girl?

There was this girl at my school, and we were getting really close. Basically, what I did wrong was I let my emotions get to me, and I started to think of negative things and that brought my morale down. We started to talk less and less, but I just couldn't lose her. To make it worst, I started sharing all my feelings with her by texting her some emotion-filled text messages day in and day out. At first, she actually helped me by giving me advice on how to stay cool and to not freak out. As the days went by, we talked less and less, and I kept sending those pathetic text messages to her. It came to the point where I think she completely gave up on me, and she probably just wants to be friends.

Well, a few weeks later, I finally have control of all my emotions, and I'm wondering if it's even worth trying. I care about her so much, and I can't bear seeing her with someone else. I know that I can definitely make her my girlfriend when I control my emotions, but I feel that she doesn't want anything to do with me at all. What I'm doing now is just waiting for her because it's summertime, and I don't see her very often. I need advice, because now she's ignoring my text messages, and I'm not panicking, but the wait is killing me, and I know if I keep waiting, something bad is going to happen, and I'll never be able to get her ever again.

I need advice, and just to clarify, if you knew me, you would know that I'm not weird or creepy or anything like that. I'm relatively popular in high school, and I played on the high school hockey team and stuff.

I just got overwhelmed with emotions, and I know I definitely should not have shared everything with her, but what do I do now? I need her.

ANSWER

A few weeks later you have total control of your emotions? Basically overnight you're a different guy?

Nope. And she's never going to believe it.

That fact that you're feeling better doesn't suddenly mean you're Mr. Composure.

What she needs to see is you in a situation where you would normally be upset and crazy, but instead you're calm and awesome.

One GREAT way to show her you've mellowed out and matured a little, is by NOT texting her, especially if she's been ignoring them.

The fact that you wrote "I can't stand to think of her with someone else" makes you sound uncomposed and delusional.

Don't beat yourself up. Life is about learning and growing up, not about chasing girls who don't want to be with you.
Take some time to mourn the loss of this great girl and learn from it. That way, you won't scare away the next great girl who wanders into your life. And trust me, no other girl is going to think you're awesome when you're still crying over your past girl. Heal up and move on. You're probably an awesome dude, so act like it.

DOES IGNORING GIRLS REALLY WORK?

QUESTION

So if I am kinda dating someone, should I be busy sometimes when she is available to do things? I'm a firefighter and have a very busy life; she's a nurse and is busy too. So if I'm busy sometimes, will she make me a bigger priority in her life? Or will it backfire? I'd like to see her more often, but I want her to instigate our encounters from time to time.

ANSWER

I think what you're really asking is "Can I see her more often without scaring her away because I get the feeling she's not as into me as I am into her?"

Am I close?

To which I might say, "This is an attraction problem, mixed with an insecurity you have about losing her."

It's typical and it sucks. Wanting someone more then they want you, or to have it at least seem that way, sucks. I've lived this nightmare plenty of times.

Mirror Her Interest Levels

Seeing her more often isn't going to scare her away unless she already doesn't want to hang out with you. Plus, it depends on how long you've been dating... a few weeks (stick to a few visits a week) or a few months (3 or 4 visits a week is okay).

The reason some women run away when a guy wants to hang out more often is because it can come across as both too needy (from him) and too much commitment (for her.) If she's unsure about you, seeing more of you isn't going to help her. Only seeing less of you works.

Less helps her miss you.

More might make her feel smothered, which will push her away. That's something you're going to have to feel out for yourself. Basically, just mirror her emotional connection to you.

If she's leaning into you emotionally, you can see her a little more.

If she's leaning away, give her more space.

Women Like It When You Lead

It's okay to ALWAYS be the initiator.

Trust me, it's OKAY.

Some women simply won't call a guy and make plans. Making plans is kind of a "masculine" thing—it's about taking action and having direction. Women love that type of guy. It's not needy, it's about being a leader and someone she feels safe with.

The only time you need to initiate less is if she's always finding reasons to say no to you. If you find she's always too busy to meet up, call her 50% less often. Eventually she'll either leave (because she wasn't into you anyway) OR she'll start calling more often, which is a win.

Chasing the girl works, but only if she lets you catch her. Don't chase a girl who's never going to be interested in getting caught.

Be Patient

It's okay to be nervous and excited to see her. It's not okay if you let that energy turn sour and needy by calling her too often and asking her how she "feels" about you, etc.

If she's having a good time with you, but only once a week, that's still a great sign!

Sometimes it can take a woman months before she's relaxed and comfortable being with you. Some women have negative past experiences with dudes and want a lot of space at the beginning of a relationship, so give her space AND be very present and fun when you're together.

BEST WAY TO APPROACH A GIRL?

QUESTION

What's the best way for a guy to approach a girl? Is there a way which doesn't appear too creepy? What about online?

ANSWER

1) Direct Is Fastest

If you're looking for speed, I recommend a "direct" approach, something you can deliver quickly, that implies you're interested but also gives you the breathing room to walk away if she's crazy.

> **YOU:** *"Excuse me, I'm not sure if I should be doing this, but you TOTALLY seem my type... but I've heard Red Heads are notorious for being angry and great ball busters. Is there any truth to that?"*

What you're saying is, "Hey, I dig your style, but I'm not totally sold yet... sell yourself a little more..." This tells her you're ballsy enough to say "hi" but not so over the top that you're Low Value. And putting a time constraint on your interaction helps make her relax because she knows you're not looking to hang around and eat up her time.

> **YOU:** *"Unfortunately I'm in a hurry to be somewhere but I just HAD to come over and say hi. I shouldn't be doing this*

*because I hear Red Heads have fiery tempers but you total-
ly seem my type and I love a woman who's passionate. My
name's Robert; it's nice to meet you."*

2) Indirect allows more time

An indirect approach allows you more time to explore her personality before getting her number AND invites her to puzzle
whether you're cool or not. It adds a tiny bit of mystery and
playfulness. A good indirect approach is to simply start a conversation with her and, over time, start to flirt.

Here's an example in a clothing store change area:

> **YOU:** *"Excuse me, do you work here? No? Oh, well, perhaps
> you can help me anyway. Do these jeans make my ass look
> fat? I need a girl's opinion."*

A Facebook (non-dating social website) example might be:

> **YOU:** *"Hey, I totally don't know you, but you have awesome
> fashion sense and I need a girl's opinion on something...
> unfortunately, all my guy friends don't get fashion, so I'm
> desperate. Any who... if I wear white shoes with my jeans do
> I HAVE to also wear a white belt? I'm not entirely sure I can
> sell the 'white belt and white shoes' look...*
>
> *Thanks in advance, Robby.*
>
> *P.S. Are you wearing leg warmers in that photo!?"*

3) Creepy guys lack calibration

The typical creepy guy stares without smiling or only sees women
as meat. And women can pick up on this a mile away.

Practice and experience chatting and being friendly with as many people as possible. Being non-creepy comes from your delivery and intent. Make your delivery "fun" and your intent "sincere."

If your intent is to meet her and have fun, you'll never seem creepy.

If your intent is to get laid, you might come across as creepy.

4) Practice

In order to not come across as creepy, you need to practice your delivery. And practice means you're going to have to start talking to EVERYONE you meet: guys, girls, old people, ugly people, etc.

Awkward dudes who don't know how to relax during a conversation are the ones who get labeled "creepy." It's mostly because they don't smile or laugh or have social calibration, and all of those things come from practice and experience.

So come up with some opening line and start using it on everyone you meet while out shopping.

While shopping in the grocery store:

> **YOU:** *"Excuse me... I'm totally out of my element here... do you know the difference between a Yam and Sweet Potato? I can't figure it out..."*

or

While shopping at the mall:

> **YOU:** *"Hey, you girls look like you have your selves really together! Can I get your insight on a fashion dilemma I have? If I buy white shoes, no sneakers, to wear with my casual*

jeans, does that mean I HAVE to wear a white belt too?!
Because I just don't know if I can pull off a white belt... I'm
confused..."

or

Restaurant:

> **YOU:** *"Do you girls eat here often? Ha! That totally sounded*
> *like a super smooth pickup line! Ignore that first sentence...*
> *any way, what I'm really wondering is if you've ever had the*
> *steak here. Is it any good?"*

or

> **YOU:** *"Hey, do I have to wear a necklace with this shirt? Is*
> *it too much chest? I'm trying to avoid the douchbag look..."*

You get the idea.

You'll be surprised how people like talking and giving their opinion.

Then, once you're super comfortable opening up to a girl or group of girls, you need to learn how to escalate. Banter transitions to flirting.

Eventually, you're going to have to express your interest in her—that's the only way to get her out on that first date.

FINAL THOUGHTS

READ THIS FIRST

A Letter To Myself

I once wrote a blog post where I magically travelled back in time to give my young insecure self some life advice.

This is that post.

If you've ever struggled with women, if you've ever been frustrated with how your life is panning out, or if you just don't know where to start then START HERE!

Dear Robert,

I'm you, from the future.

That's fucked up, right?

I know.

Most people might assume I'm joking, but I know that you'll be just curious enough to hear me out.

How do I know?

Because I'm you... from the future, remember?

Yup, I'm you except 20 years older, 50 pounds fatter, and much, MUCH wiser.

I've magically sent you this letter from the future for a reason... I want you to learn from my dating mistakes.

I want you to have some dating success while you're still young enough to make the most of it!

And, well, I've always wondered how my life would be different if I "just got it" before going through a divorce and entering my 30s confused. And by "got it," I'm implying a deeper appreciation of women and the complexities of dating dynamics.

Will you still grow up into a dude who's

fascinated by women and dating and sex and relationships if you don't live a life full of the same painful memories I have?

I don't know, but I'm willing to take that chance. So pay attention; I have very little time to type this up...

DATING ADVICE TO MYSELF

1) RELAX

How old are you now, Robby? 13?

I'm guessing you're still freaking out about your last girlfriend... the one who was trying to have sex with you at her all-girl party?

Well let me just say this... Relax.

You're gonna get laid eventually, so don't rush yourself. Just be proud that you walked away without being too molested. ;)

Take the next few years to learn how to meditate. Not only will it improve your mood, your sleeping patterns, and your ability to think, puzzle solve, and focus, it'll also improve your self esteem, your ability to stay composed in the face of excitement (or embarrassment), AND girls will not rock your emotional centre so easily.

Instead you'll be as cool as a cucumber, and

girls love cucumbers.

2) STOP SEEKING APPROVAL

I know it seems like all of the popular girls know exactly what they want and how to get it. I know it seems like they are all ignoring you despite your best efforts.

But they're not.

They're just distracted by the intense insecurities they have about themselves. EVERYONE IS!

While you're sitting at home feeling too skinny (dude, I haven't felt too skinny since I was your age... what I would give to feel too skinny again...) you need to relax and realize that these same girls are endlessly reading makeup and gossip magazines desperately trying to get everyone else's approval.

That super cute girl in class?

She goes home and worries about being too skinny or too tall or too fat or too zitty or too hairy or too short or too ugly or too loud or too smart... etc.

All she wants is for everyone to like her.

I know it doesn't seem this way. I know it seems like she doesn't care at all. But she does.

I KNOW she does.

I mean, just ask any girl in your class what she worries most about. You'll discover that she's hoping for some other person's approval (her parents, or best friend, her teacher, that cute guy in class, etc.)

The trick of seeming super confident (which is every guy's goal who's trying to get the girl) is to STOP seeking everyone else's approval.

I didn't realize until later in life (and I still struggle with this) that what other people think of you doesn't matter.

Read that again.

It doesn't MATTER what other people think of you.

The only person you're accountable to, ultimately, is yourself.

When you sleep at night, the only person who can judge you in a real sense is yourself.

So simply do what YOU think is best (it's okay to ask others for advice but make all your decisions yourself) because when you make mistakes, it's your fault, and when you achieve great things, it's also your fault.

Take responsibility for yourself and stop seeking the approval of others.

Others don't matter when it comes to YOUR life, so make your own decisions.
Besides, every time you seek some girl's approval, you'll come across as weak, limp, and gross.

Don't be gross.

And don't seek her approval.

Let her seek YOUR approval.

What you'll discover is that everyone, once you stop seeking their approval, will start seeking yours.

It's amazing.

Other kids will try to goof-off you by teasing you about your acne or your skinny arms, but the moment they realize you don't care is the same moment they lose all their power.

You see, when you react and get upset from the "words" of some buffoon, you send the message that you're weak and easy to manipulate. You give the buffoon power and attention.

And everyone wants attention.

So instead of arguing with these idiots, ignore

them or, at the very most, simply agree. It's hard for someone else to argue with you when you agree with them.

For example, that tall hockey player in class who's trying to impress his girlfriend by calling your hair style too girly?
Just agree.

Try something like, "I know, right!? My hair is soooo girl. I was just wearing it this silly way because I go home at night worried about what you think of me. "

Being sarcastic is another great tool by the way.

Another easy response? "Ya, totally, right? Ya, you're right. You're totally right."

Let's try it.

Random Asshole: "Hey Rob, try lifting some weights ... your arms are like twigs!"

You: "Ya, totally, right? Ya, you're right. You're totally right." or "Whatever dude. My arms are awesome."

My point? Don't be that guy who's always trying to get people to like him. You're better than that.

3) DON'T TAKE THINGS PERSONALLY.

You're skinny, ugly, and nobody likes you.

But don't take it personally.

Easier said than done, right?

Well, it's a powerful practice that'll free you
from endless suffering, so take this seriously.

I remember growing up and being constantly
told how to think and feel. This is how older
people control you..... by convincing you
to always seek their approval and take
everything they say to heart.

But the truth is that they aren't living in your
shoes, and they don't know what it's like to
live your life. So be willing to hear the advice of
others, but make your own decisions.

And realize that everything everyone else says
about you or to you has nothing to do with
you, really. It's always got something to do with
them.

That dude who's picking on you in class?

It's got nothing to do with you. He's the
outcome of 13 years growing up with an
asshole father and older brothers who beat
him up. He's lashing out at you because he's
trying to find a way to feel better about
himself.

It's got nothing to do with you. Besides, he
doesn't even know you, so how can he be any
kind of judge regarding you or your actions?

Try this on for size: Ignore all compliments anyone gives you.
WHAT?

Yes.

Because if you allow the compliments of others to affect how you see yourself, you're also going to be willing to accept their insults as well.

Ultimately, your goal is to ignore all judgments about you.

Why? Because you want the only judge in your life to be you ... all other judgments can be ignored or, at the very most, seen as critical feedback.

If everyone hates you, take it as good feedback.

It means you're doing something that's making them uncomfortable ... It's a good time to evaluate what you're doing.

This doesn't mean they're right; it just means they're giving you feedback.

When that super hot Red Head in class laughs at the love letter you wrote her and shares it with her friends, that's the perfect time to practice this idea ... don't take it personally.

It's got nothing to do with you.

She's not REALLY trying to hurt you or embarrass you. She's simply unsure how to react. All she knows is that she shares everything with her friends and therefore HAS to share your love note with them.
The lesson here?

Don't waste time on love letters unless you're already dating.

Instead, flirt, have fun, and stay away from trying to "logic" her into liking you.

Did your best friend call you 'stupid' and 'unlikable'?

Doesn't matter.

He doesn't REALLY know you ... he can't really know your true thoughts and feelings; therefore, everything he says about you doesn't matter because he doesn't have the background or authority to make those judgments.

He's just saying mean things because he's embarrassed or mad or sad.

Everyone else does everything they do because of them not because of you.

4) STOP JUDGING YOURSELF

Now that you're realizing the judgment of

others is all bullshit, it's time to Realize one
other thing ... your own judgments are bullshit.

Every time you get mad at yourself you're
hurting yourself, and that's not what makes a
boy a man.

A man comes from maturity and love not
from anger and hatred and self-judgment.

There's Real science to this next statement
... all of those voices in your head that are
helping or hurting you come from your mom,
grandma, teachers, and preachers.

Those people who were most present in our
lives growing up? It's their voices we now have
in our heads.

We're basically little computers programmed
by our parents.

And it takes many years to learn this.

That voice that says, "Hey, don't do that!
That's wrong!" isn't you, it's the voice of your
mom from your youth.

We all have this problem.

We all have early programming in our heads
that we think is US, but it's not.

It's something we agreed to because we didn't
have the personal power to challenge the

thoughts and ideas of our parents. We didn't have the problem-solving skills. So they teach us as best as they can, but then we forget.

We forget that most of these ideas aren't our own-they're the ideas of our church, school, or peers.

Therefore, you can't always trust your own thoughts until you've taken the time to LEARN which ones are truly your own and which are the opinions of your parents.

Learn how to challenge your own thoughts, especially painful or negative ones.

Do you have thoughts that make you sad or embarrassed or mad?
Those are the thoughts you need to challenge.

Does it REALLY matter if you're skinny, or you didn't get that higher grade, or that Sally doesn't like you?
Does it?

Or are you just thinking up stuff to give yourself a reason to feel sorry for yourself?

Is your ego so weak and pathetic that you need to always be right? Maybe it's actually okay to be wrong. Maybe that's how we grow up-by being wrong a lot. Maybe that's not bad or embarrassing ... maybe that's growing and learning and becoming awesome.

That type of negative self-judgment isn't what will make you into a strong, happy man. It'll only weaken and depress you.

Everyone has these challenges, so don't fret.

Nobody teaches us how to grow up thinking positive happy thoughts. Instead, we're taught to feel guilty about everything and to fear everything.

This is wrong.

Nothing I've ever really feared has brought me happiness or confidence.

Have some awareness of your own thoughts. There's a lot of judging going on in there–turn it off.

It's okay to fail sometimes.

It's okay to say the wrong thing from time to time.

It's okay to masturbate!

All the weird negative stuff you gathered into your head from listening to others ... make sure it really DOES make sense before you keep it.

Just like you used to believe in Santa Claus?

You did so because you didn't question things

enough.

So ignore others and only ask questions that help you, not hinder you.

5) KEEP DOING WHAT YOU LOVE

Your passions for art and playing with friends and keeping fit are all things that make others want to be around you. It's your personal passions that people find interesting, so keep that up.

It's what makes you so interesting.

And interesting is what get's the girl. It's what brings joy into your day.

This all goes back to approval seeking. There are too many teenagers doing what their parents tell them to do.

Some guys are becoming doctors because dad said so.

Some girls are becoming models because they desperately want people to like them.

But happiness comes from within, not from the approval of others.

Do what you like; don't question whether others like it or not.

Trust me, it's this type of thinking that makes leaders. Leaders are people who go where they want, and others follow.

6) BE SOCIAL

People are fascinating.

They've lived lives you haven't. They make decisions you might not. And they have motivations you might not understand. And the only way to learn that is by being open, honest, sincere, and friendly with everyone you meet.

The key to making friends with strangers is to be a good listener while being curious about them instead of busily trying to talk about yourself.

Allowing people to talk about themselves encourages them to open up to you when they won't open up to others, and that's powerful.

And the less you judge them, the more they'll love you for it.

(Plus, we judge ourselves the way we judge others, so stop yourself from calling one guy fat or some girl ugly. These are useless judgments that will damage your inner peace and calm.)

Want to draw people to you? Listen; don't judge;

be curious.

If you have stories you MUST share, save them
for close friends. Don't burden each new
stranger with your desperate desire to share
your stories. It's needy and approval-seeking,
and people hate that.

Instead, just be a good listener. And be curious.
The Number 1 skill you should develop is your
social skills.

Learning how to make small talk with people
will introduce you to some really beautiful girls.
While every other guy gets nervous around hot
girls, you'll be calm and normal.

Why?

Because you're not seeking her approval, you're
just being normal and fun.

And the fastest way to become socialized like
this is through social interactions. So learn
to make small talk with everyone you meet...
while shopping, while at school, while walking or
biking, etc.

Just learn how to be social and friendly.

You don't have to wow people. You don't have to
be super interesting. You just have to be able to
make small talk.

From there, you'll learn how to share funny

jokes you've seen or heard. And from there, you'll always have something funny to say to any hot girls you meet.

Like that girl at 7-11 you were afraid to talk to.

Or that girl in the bikini who walked over to say hi but you sheepishly said nothing.

It takes time, and it takes patience, but the pay-off is ridiculously powerful.

Being good with people is the greatest skill you can ever learn.

7) HAVE COMPASSION

This is my final thought. All of my above suggestions lead to this one idea.

Life should be fun and not too serious.

Realize that everyone has his or her own trials and struggles. And all they want is for others to like them and give them approval.

So as you're learning to grow and mature and take care of yourself, you'll find you're strong enough to help lift others up as well.

Don't just dismiss people because they're less cool or because they're angry and jaded.

Instead, realize they have faults they don't see;

sometimes other people just need someone who's willing to lend an ear. Maybe you can lend that ear.

Sometimes people are hurting and simply need to be heard in order to feel better.

So while you're learning how to have fun and appreciate yourself, realize that sometimes it feels good to help others, too.

Be compassionate and caring; it'll invite other passionate and caring people into your life. Care for yourself and then start to care for others.

It'll pay off, I swear.

See you soon,

~ Robby

RESOURCES & LINKS

LINKS

GET THE GIRL - VIDEO COURSE (50% OFF):

   ✍ **http://members.ignoreandscore.com/?couponcode=BOOK50**

BOOK RESOURCES:

   ✍ **www.IgnoreAndScore.com**

ATTRACTION RESOURCES:

   ✍ **www.IgnoreAndScore.com/attraction**

LEADING RESOURCES:

   ✍ **www.IgnoreAndScore.com/leading**

RAPPORT RESOURCES:

   ✍ **www.IgnoreAndScore.com/rapport**

ESCALATION RESOURCES:

www.IgnoreAndScore.com/escalation

MY DATING ADVICE BLOG:

www.FullOfHateAndReadyToDate.com

I SOMETIMES ANSWER DATING QUESTIONS HERE:

www.girlsaskguys.com/user/bobair/Answers

FOLLOW ME ON TWITTER:

twitter.com/robertbelland

SEND QUESTIONS OR COMPLAINTS HERE:

questions@IgnoreAndScore.com

56178731R00115

Made in the USA
Middletown, DE
20 July 2019